Better Living with Astrology and Tarot

Larry Coleman

©2011 Larry Coleman. All rights reserved.
ISBN 978-1-257-77725-9

Contents

Acknowledgments   v

Introduction   vii

I   Fundamentals   1

1 The Concepts   3
    1.1 Numerology 3
    1.2 The Four Worlds 5
    1.3 The Elements 6
    1.4 The Planets 7
    1.5 The Zodiac 9
    1.6 Eris and the Golden Apple 11

2 Meet the Source   13

II   Strategy   19

3 Introduction to Astrology   21
    3.1 Chart Points 22
    3.2 Houses 23
    3.3 The Planets 26

3.4	Major Asteroids	28
3.5	The Signs	29
3.6	Aspects	31
3.7	You're Every Sign!	33

4 Your Birth Chart — 35
- 4.1 Obtaining Your Birth Chart 35
- 4.2 Intepreting Your Chart 36
  - 4.2.1 Personality and Life Purpose 36
  - 4.2.2 Relationships 40
  - 4.2.3 Vocation 41
- 4.3 Other Life Areas 42
- 4.4 Development Planning 45
  - 4.4.1 Aspects 47
- 4.5 When to Seek Professional Help 48

5 Transits and Progressions — 51
- 5.1 Progressions 52
- 5.2 Transits 53

6 The Solar Return — 59
- 6.1 Annual Profection 60
- 6.2 Yearly Progressions 62
- 6.3 Yearly Transits 63

III Tactics — 67

7 Introduction to Tarot — 69

8 The Minor Arcana — 73
- 8.1 Overview of the System 73
- 8.2 Wands 75
- 8.3 Cups 79
- 8.4 Swords 83

	8.5 Pentacles	86
9	**The Major Arcana**	**91**
10	**How to Do a Reading**	**103**
	10.1 Recipe for a Helpful Reading	103
	10.2 The Celtic Cross	105
	10.3 Sample Celtic Cross Spread	107
	10.4 Reading for Others	109

Acknowledgments

Acknowledgments I would like to thank the following people, in no particular order:

- My parents
- My friends at B.O.T.A.
- The Detroit Area Tarot Guild
- The Sun Conjunct Uranus astrology group
- Chris Brennan, whose Hellenistic Astrology course showed me the underlying simplicity of astrology
- Nancy Cross for providing initial editing help
- Everyone who has ever seen me at a restaurant or coffee house and asked: "What are you reading?"

Introduction

My name is Larry, and I'm a recovering materialist.

By materialism I mean the belief that the material world as known to science is all there is, or at least all that is important. I use the word recovering because I'm not sure that we ever get completely away from materialism, and that may not even be the point of us being here.

Ten years ago, I was an atheist, and a fundamentalist materialist. I read cognitive science books claiming that consciousness was a phenomenon that emerged from the interaction of neural activity. I read other books that claimed that since there is no possible observable difference between a world with a God and a world without a God, the term "God" was therefore meaningless. And I was happy in my materialist cave.

Then September 11 happened. I spent a few months trying to make sense of everything but the official story just wasn't working for me. One day I stumbled on a metaphysical sort of book about September 11. Now there I was given a story that worked. Unfortunately, the story came bundled with conspiracy theory and references to extra-dimensional lizards. You take the part that's useful, right?

Besides providing a better explanation of the September 11 events, the book also introduced me to the concept of a holographic universe. You may be familiar with the hologram as a three-dimensional picture. A hologram is made by splitting a laser beam and bouncing one part off the subject of the picture, for example an apple, then combining it with the other half. Shining a laser through the resulting film creates the picture. If someone cut the film in half, you would expect to see a picture of half an apple. What happens is that you see a smaller, fuzzier picture of the whole apple. What this implies is that each half of the film has information about the entire picture.

The holographic universe theory says that the universe has the same property, that each part of it has information about the rest. We will be making extensive use of this theory during the course of the book.

At the time, I found the holographic universe metaphor interesting, and even read a book about it. I also read more about quantum physics, and noticed that the most advanced physicists almost all had mystical leanings. I also read *The Tao of Physics*. Taoism and Buddhism have in common the lack of a personal God, and were therefore non-threatening for a then-committed atheist. Thus started a decade-long journey toward spirituality.

A milestone on the journey was watching a movie named "What the Bleep Do We Know?" This movie explored quantum physics and new discoveries in neurobiology and their implications in our daily lives. This movie started a side journey for me into the manifestation movement. This movement is about changing our thought patterns in order to change the results we see in our daily lives. I'm still an advocate of manifestation, but there's work that needs to be done before we can manifest things most effectively. Some of this work involves becoming more familiar with what we want and need, as opposed to what we think we should want. The other thing we may need to do is reprogram our subconscious minds to remove things that block our progress.

However, the most important things may be to update our model of how the universe works and to reconsider our views on what is and what is not possible.

That update started for me when I signed up for a class on Reiki, which is a Japanese form of energy balancing. In one of the exercises in the class, each person was given a name by someone else in the course. Using a technique given in the class, we were supposed to tell something about the physical condition of the person whose name we were given. The classmate who gave the name would then verify the description. Everyone in the class was able to find out something about a person they had never seen.

I learned that tarot and astrology do work. That would have been unthinkable to the person I was ten years ago. With those tools, I've done readings where things have come out that no one else knew. The cards that showed up reflected what was on the mind of the person I was doing the reading for; in fact, I found this happening so often that if it didn't happen, I considered the reading to be a failure. I spent some time back-testing astrological indicators of current influences, and discovered that many of the major events in my life could have been predicted. More importantly, I learned that none of us are one-dimensional. We all have infinite potential; most of us, however, are uncomfortable admitting out potential and even less comfortable living up to that potential.

The last leg of the journey involved a branch of astrology known as horary, where a chart is drawn up in response to a question based on the time and place the question was received. I was asked a question was about a lost box and I was able to answer the question accurately. This type of astrology is incompatible with the materialist worldview, and my interest in it is the surest measure of how far the journey has taken me.

The book in your hands was conceived at a meeting of a local tarot group. In a discussion about the correspondences between zodiac signs and the court cards (who you'll meet later) someone asked if there were any books with detailed information about this. None of us could come up with a good answer. A couple of days later, I was thinking that there really should be a book about that.

What I aim to accomplish with this book is to lay out a plan for personal and spiritual development using Tarot and Astrology as tools. Tarot and Astrology are both intricate topics, and covering both in one book may seem intimidating, however, the same basic concepts are used for both. What I will show you in this book is how to build up intepretations in both Tarot and Astrology from the basic concepts, and then what to do about those interpretations.

By reading this book, you will be starting a journey of your own. I can't tell you what's at the end of the road. I can tell you that life is more meaningful and rich while walking the Path. I've met some great people along the way, and learned a lot about them and about myself.

This book is divided into three parts. Part I explains basic concepts that we will use as a foundation for our work. In Chapter 1 you'll learn about things like the Four Elements, the Zodiac Signs and Planets, and some Numerology[1]. In Chapter 2 we'll talk more about the holographic universe and how you can interact with it for fun and profit. You'll also learn about manifestation, what it is, and two different styles of it.

Part II covers the use of astrology for long-term planning of personal development. In Chapter 4 you'll learn how to obtain and interpret your birth chart, and how to use this information to make a long-term plan for personal development. In Chapter 5, you'll learn how to track celestial influences on your life. Chapter 6 covers planning on a yearly basis around the celestial influences expected during the year.

Part III is devoted to the use of Tarot for day-to-day guidance and brainstorming. Chapter 7 will give you some basic information about the Tarot deck, how it's organized, and what it's used for. Chapters 8 and 9 will cover interpretations of the cards. In Chapter 10, you'll learn how to use them to do readings for yourself and others. You'll also learn more about what Tarot is good at and not so good at.

You need not worry that this book will put professional astrologers and Tarot readers out of business. If you're like most people, you'll find that doing these things for yourself is just too much work. Most people, for example, know how to change their oil in their cars, but have a professional do it because it's faster and

---

[1] You'll also learn why I capitalized all those words

there's no cleanup to deal with. Knowing the basic concepts will help you get more out of astrology and tarot readings that you pay for. The reader or astrologer won't have to explain the concepts, and will have more time for identifying and resolving issues.

Part I
Fundamentals

Chapter 1

The Concepts

I've been studying Astrology and Tarot extensively for the last couple of years, and I've discovered that both are based on combinations of simple basic concepts. I won't just be giving you "laundry lists" of different combinations and what they mean. Instead, I will give you the tools to construct the laundry lists yourself. Specifically, I will introduce you to the basic concepts and give some examples of how they combine to produce the complex meanings found in Astrology and Tarot.

1.1 Numerology

Numerology, as you may expect from the name, is the study of Numbers. The capitalization is to point out that Numbers in numerology are not the same as numbers in mathematics or general life. On the other hand, they are derived from numbers in general life. For example, there's a number called the Life Path Number, which is derived from your birth date. There's another number called the Destiny Number, which is derived from your full name.

Numerology is the core of Tarot, and is key to understanding the Tree of Life. A complete treatment of numerology is beyond the scope of the book, but some basic information about characteristics of the base numbers will be helpful later. I've included a couple of numerology books in the Bibliography for those who would like to learn about the subject.

Zero Zero is not used as a Base Number in numerology, but is a very important concept (western civilization would not exists as we know it today without the zero), and it is very useful in interpreting some of the Major Arcana Tarot cards.

A key meaning of Zero is potential. A current theory in physics says that what we know as empty space is actually full of energy, and particles can be created from this energy at any time. With that in mind, Zero can best be described as the void from which all things are created. Remember this when we get to the Wheel of Fortune and Judgment, two Tarot cards you will meet later.

One Individuality and beginnings are obvious meanings of the Number One, but think also about the concentration of the universal consciousness into a single point (Hint: that's you). See also the active modality below.

Two Duplication and polarity are obvious meanings of the Number Two. Also consider companionship, and the continuation of what was started by One. Also the passive modality below.

Three Growth and multiplication. See also the integrating modality below.

Four Stabilization and order, regulation and management.

Five Adjustment and adaptation, also tearing down structures created by Four.

Six Equilibrium between the forces of Four and Five, also harmony and symmetry.

Seven Creation and multiplication of abstractions.

Eight Implementation and concrete details.

Nine Completion, fulfillment.

Ten Ten is not a Base Number, but has some useful meanings for Tarot. It is the beginning of a new cycle with the just-finished cycle as a basis. It is also the meanings of One expressed through the void of Zero. More about this when we discuss the Wheel of Fortune.

1.2 The Four Worlds

The Four Worlds is a concept we will borrow from a symbol system called Qabala. They are really more accurately thought of as stages of development or manifestation, as you'll see from the descriptions, but other writers who cover topics like those in this book refer to them as the Four Worlds, so you should be familiar with the term.

Each of the stages is more specific than the last, and builds on what has been done in the last. The end result of the four stages is that something is different about the world.

Archetypal World This stage of creation consists of the seed on an idea. It's nothing specific at this point, just a general though of making or doing something.

Creative World This stage of creation directs the creative impulse given above into a specific direction. In this stage, you can also feel the excitement of a new idea and about the results.

Formative World In this stage of creation, specific details about the idea are worked out. Brainstorming is common, followed by selecting the best items from the brainstorming results.

Manifested World This is the final stage of creation, and the only stage that has tangible results. The actual thing is done or made in this stage.

To illustrate the four stages, suppose you'd like to build a house. The idea of building a house is like the first stage or Archetypal World. Looking at different house styes and considering different locations is like the second stage or Creative World. Selecting pre-printed plans for the house or hiring an architect, and selecting a specific location, is like the third stage or Formative World. Building the house and moving in is like the fourth stage or Manifested World.

Each stage is more specific or differentiated than the last. Also, making changes to the design of a house is a lot less expensive in the second stage than the fourth. This property will be useful to us when we talk about manifestation later.

You may have noticed from the descriptions above that most of the activity doesn't take place where someone can see it. That's part of the model. The universe in general is mostly stuff we can't see. We'll talk about this more in Chapter 2.

1.3 The Elements

At the time of this writing, the periodic table lists 118 elements. This section is not about any of them. An Element from our perspective is more like a principle or a force. In this work I will use "Element" to refer to one of the four below, and we won't need to discuss the other type.

Fire △ Fire is associated with spirit, consciousness, energy, and initiative. In Tarot, Fire corresponds to the suit Wands. Fire corresponds also to the Archetypal World in the previous section.

Water ▽ Water is associated with emotions and the subconscious. In Tarot, Water corresponds to the suit Cups. Water also corresponds to the Creative World in the previous section.

Air △ Air is associated with thoughts, beliefs, communication, and justice. In Tarot, Air corresponds to the suit Swords. Air also corresponds to the Formative World in the previous section.

6

Earth ▽ Earth is associated with physical manifestation and the material world. In Tarot, Earth corresponds to the suit Pentacles. Earch also corresponds to the Manifested World above.

Fire and Air are both active, while Water and Earth are passive. Fire and Water unify, while Air and Earth draw distinctions.

Another interesting way of looking at the four elements is given by Demetra George [2]: she associates Fire with freedom, Water with security, Air with change, and Earth with stability. It's an interesting association because striking balances between those four elements seems to be the central issue of politics, as well as life in general. We will be using both sets of associations in this work.

1.4 The Planets

Some people think of myths as being equivalent to fairy tales. Another opinion is that they are allegories for things that are difficult to explain without them. I will present an alternate viewpoint here.

The gods and goddesses of old are alive and well, but not in the way you might think. They are internal, and are actually parts of ourselves that we may not recognize or honor. We will be referring to them here as "Planets." Part of my job here will be to acquaint you with them and to show you how to connect with them and atone for any neglect that may have occurred.

Astrology provides a model of the psyche, as does mythology. The world *psyche* is Greek and could be translated as "mind" or "soul." It really refers to the person as a whole, including the body, at least under the model we'll be using in this book. How mythology and astrology work together is that mythology tells stories that illustrate the principles given by astrology. Under this model, the planets in astrology correspond to capacities or functions.

Sun ☉ Apollo is the Roman Sun god. He is traditionally very charismatic, and good with poetry and music, but for some reason doesn't have much luck with women. The sun represents basic identity, life purpose, and the ego, which may have been why the ancients considered the Sun not to be very beneficial. It hides any planet that is too close to it; similarly the ego can hide other parts of the personality and typically does so on a regular basis.

Moon ☽ Isis is a good example of a traditional moon goddess. Mother Nature is also a good correspondence. The moon represents emotional responses, habits, and the body. Since the moon is mainly visible at night, it's a good metaphor for processes that operate inside us under the surface.

Mercury ☿ Mercury was the messenger of the gods, and as a Planet represents learning habits and communication styles, and interaction with the immediate environment in general. A good talk show host would exemplify qualities of Mercury.

Venus ♀ Venus, the goddess of love, attracts valued things and people, especially love and money. This is not always a good thing, as Paris of Troy would tell you if he were here. Venus simply attracts what is desired; whether the object of desire is something beneficial or worth having is a question for another planet; Saturn is better at that sort of thing. More details later in the chapter.

Mars ♂ Mars, the god of war, represents self-assertion and action toward goals. Football players, especially linebackers, are good examples of the Mars quality in people. A linebacker has a simple goal: find the man carrying the football and knock him over; if anyone gets in your way, deal with him as needed. People who are expressing the mars quality pursue their goals and deal with whoever stands in the way.

Jupiter ♃ Jupiter, the head of the Roman pantheon, represents expansion, improvement, and the "big picture." Jupiter is probably most famous for having many children, mostly with women other than his wife. The metaphor here is that expansive thinking can make you very productive and creative. Santa Claus is another popular Jupiter archetype.

Saturn ♄ Saturn, Jupiter's deposed father, represents restriction, responsibility and focus. Just between you and me, Saturn is really still running things. He just prefers to concentrate on important things and leave the rest to Jupiter. If you've ever tried to do something you shouldn't, and been prevented by unforeseen events, you've witnessed Saturn at work. Other Saturn archetypes include Father Time and the Grim Reaper.

I've left out the other three planets for now. They definitely have roles, but not of the same type as those listed above. For now, we'll say that if Jupiter is the figurehead leader while Saturn really runs things, the outer three planets would be the "shadow government." We'll discuss the outer planets when we talk about your scheduled growth program.

1.5 The Zodiac

The zodiac in astronomy is a set of constellations. In astrology, the Zodiac is a division of the Sun's apparent orbit around the Earth into twelve sections based on the seasons. For example, Aries starts on the first day of spring in the Northern Hemisphere. This is by definition. Similarly, the Sun enters Cancer on the first day of summer, Libra on the first day of autumn, and Capricorn on the first day of winter.

You are likely familiar with your Sun Sign, which is the Zodiac Sign the Sun was in at the time of your birth, but the Zodiac Sign describes operations of other planets as well. The descriptions are based on combinations of an element and quality, and are modified by the nature of the planet that rules, or is strongest in, each Sign.

What follows is a listing of each sign with descriptions of its components. Once you see how the components fit together, you'll understand why the signs have the characteristics they do. For example, you'll understand why Virgos have reputations for being critical.

♈ **Aries** Aries is a Cardinal Fire Sign ruled by Mars. Cardinal Fire in our system means initiating or creating freedom and identity, in this case in an assertive manner due to the Mars influence.

♉ **Taurus** Taurus is a Fixed Earth Sign ruled by Venus. Fixed Earth in our system means maintaining or continuing physical security. Since Taurus is ruled by Venus, the physical security will be in the form of nice things.

♊ **Gemini** Gemini is a Mutable Air Sign ruled by Mercury. Mutable Air in our system means evaluating and distributing ideas and changes, which is also the function of Mercury.

♋ **Cancer** Cancer is a Cardinal Water Sign ruled by the Moon. Cardinal Water means initiating or creating emotional security. The Moon, in addition to being in charge of emotions, is also the fastest-moving Planet.

♌ **Leo** Leo is a Fixed Fire Sign ruled by the Sun. Fixed Fire in our system means maintaining freedom and identity. The Sun rules identity, and adds warmth to the qualities of the sign.

♍ **Virgo** Virgo is a Mutable Earth Sign ruled by Mercury. Mutable Earth in our system means evaluating and distributing physical security, and Mercury is in charge of communication.

♎ **Libra** Libra is a Cardinal Air sign ruled by Venus. Cardinal Air in our system means initiating thoughts, communication and changes. Since Libra is ruled by Venus, Libra wants all of the thought and communication to be harmonious if possible.

♏ **Scorpio** Scorpio is a Fixed Water Sign ruled by Mars. Fixed Water in our system means maintaining emotional security.

Since Scorpio is ruled by Mars, the assertiveness comes out whenever the emotional security is threatened.

- ♐ **Sagittarius** Sagittarius is a Mutable Fire Sign ruled by Jupiter. Mutable Fire in our system means evaluating and distributing freedom and identity. The Jupiter rulership adds a "big picture" emphasis, along with a tendency for adventure.

- ♑ **Capricorn** Capricorn is a Cardinal Earth Sign ruled by Saturn. Cardinal Earth in our system means establishing physical security. Saturn adds structure and focus to the physical security.

- ♒ **Aquarius** Aquarius is a Fixed Air Sign ruled by Saturn. Fixed Air in our system means maintaining thoughts and communication, and Saturn adds restriction and focus.

- ♓ **Pisces** Pisces is a Mutable Water Sign ruled by Jupiter. Mutable Water in our system means evaluating and distributing emotional security, and the Jupiter rulership adds a "big picture" emphasis.

1.6 Eris and the Golden Apple

Eris was the Greek goddess of chaos. She was unpopular with the other deities, and as a result wasn't invited to a wedding party. Now a goddess of chaos isn't going to let an orderly thing like an invitation stop her, so she crashed the party and left a gift. The gift was a golden apple engraved with the words: "To the Prettiest One."

When the other deities saw the apple, there was an argument about who it was meant for. Athena (Pallas), Aphrodite (or Venus), and Hera (Juno)[1] all claimed the apple for themselves. The other gods found themselves incapable of judging the matter objectively,

---

[1] You'll meet Pallas/Athena and Juno/Hera later when we talk about asteroids.

or at least that was Zeus/Jupiter's excuse, and therefore enlisted the help of Paris, a country shepherd.

The three goddesses decided to play dirty, and each of them offered Paris a bribe. Hera offered to make Paris the most powerful man in the world. Athena offered to make him wise and the best fighter. Aphrodite offered him the companionship of the most beautiful woman in the world.

Paris apparently lacked patience and/or wisdom, so he chose Aphrodite and her reward. There was a minor sticking point: Helen of Troy was already married, and so was Paris. Aphrodite didn't care; she's the goddess of love; she'll just "make it happen."

So Helen ran off with Paris, and Helen's husband was upset enough about it to start the Trojan war. There were lots of casualties, including Paris himself, and Troy was destroyed.

Like most good myths, this one has a few lessons associated with it. The first is obvious: "Be careful what you wish for. You might get it."

The next one's a little more subtle. Paris went for Aphrodite's offer of the most beautiful woman, but had he taken Hera's offer, he would have been the most powerful man in the world, and would still have had many choices (leaving aside the fact that he was already married). He may not have been with the most beautiful woman in the world, but definitely a pretty close second. The lesson here is that a little foresight can go a long way.

The story also illustrates how conflicting impulses within us can cause us to do things that aren't in our long-term best interest. Paris was just a simple shepherd before having to make this choice. He may not have been happy, but his life was certainly a lot less stressful.

The final and most important lesson is that chaos must at least be appeased if not honored.

Chapter 2

Meet the Source

Most people think of the universe as being composed of a multitude of stars, galaxies, quasars, and the like, with mostly empty space between them. The Great Work has a different model of the universe: it's one very big thing, and it's alive. You don't have to accept this model to use the techniques given in this book, but the techniques have the model as a basis, so if you don't accept the model, you'll have to come up with your explanation about how all this works!

The idea is that astrology and Tarot work because they are based on this model, and the principle of correspondence: As Above, So Below. In other words, things that happen on the large scale are similar to things that happen on the small scale. For example, the structure of the atom has for a long time been compared to the structure of the solar system. The application of the principle that most concerns is that things that happen in the sky, or in the layout of cards, mirror things that happen inside us. This is why if you get a Tarot reading, you don't need to tell the reader why you are there; if the reading is successful, the things you are concerned about will be reflected in the cards.

As a side note, astrology and Tarot are frequent targets of what is known as the "Skeptic" community. I use quotes around the word because they are anything but skeptical; they are actually fervent believers in reductionist materialism. If astrology and Tarot work, then their worldview is invalid. So don't be fooled by their claims of objectivity.

A quick visualization may give you a general idea of what the Source is like. The more you practice this, the closer your connection will be. What I'd like you to do is find a time and place where you will not be disturbed for a few minutes. Close your eyes, and imagine a light source ahead. Imagine that the light source comes closer until it is all around you. You can feel the light not only around you, but even permeating your body. The light burns away all of your problems. Inside of the light, all of your senses are heightened, and you feel safe and secure. Stay in the light for as long as you like.

There may be an apparent conflict between the material given here and the teachings of the organized religions you know. My position is that this conflict is only apparent, though you may not want to bring up the subject matter discussed here around certain fundamentalists. Light is only one metaphor for the Source. Other names for it include God and the Universe. This metaphor is actually compatible with any religion, as the major religions all claim that God is infinite; however, adherents of those religions may not take the claim seriously. For example, an infinte God doesn't really allow for a competing power named Satan. It also doesn't allow for being separate from God, who if infinite would have to be everywhere.

One consequence of this infinity is the God is too big to fit into our heads, so we each have subsets that are at least in theory comprehensible. The problems happen when we mistake our subsets for the whole; doing this is like going to a restaurant and trying to eat the menu, then convincing yourself that it tastes good. It says "prime rib", so it has to taste good!

Part of the power of the Source is available to you to help you achieve your goals. The formula is: Idea, Desire, Details, Manifestation. The Idea part is easy; the tricky part is Desire. It's true that you have to really want the thing you are trying to achieve; but not from the standpoint of "I really really hope I get this." Instead, the approach should be "I really like this new thing and I'm grateful that it's happening." If you were paying attention during Chapter 1, you may have noticed that the formula is similar to the descriptions of the Four Elements. This similarity is intentional. The Idea is Fire; the Desire, Water; Details correspond to Air; and Manifestation to Earth.

The formula also corresponds to the Four Worlds from Chapter 1. You may remember that each of the Four Worlds is more differentiated or specific than the last. I also mentioned that making changes is easier at the less differentiated points which occur earlier in the process of creation. This implies that if you have a change you'd like to make in your life, it will be more effective if the change starts at the level of ideas (Air) or emotions (Water) instead of a brute-force approach in the physical world (Earth). As an example, if you smoke cigarettes and would like to quit, you can try just quitting cold-turkey (Earth), and that works for some people. It might be more effective to combine that with making a list of the benefits of not smoking (Air), or by getting excited about the money you'd save and the health benefits (Water). Best of all for this purpose is having something inside you decide that it's time (Fire).

When working through the Details, there are two general approaches. I'll describe them below. You'll most likely get an idea of which way will fit your needs and personality as you examine your birth chart in more detail. Both approaches involve a form of meditation given by the exercise discussed above. For best results, perform the meditation multiple times.

If you use the first approach, you will imagine the desired result in as much detail as possible. In the following days, you will take whatever actions you think will help you progress toward your goal. This approach gives you the benefit of having a picture imprinted on your subconscious, which may reduce any internal resistance. We will call this approach the Way of the Magician.

If you use the second approach, you will imagine how you will feel when you have the desired result. That's all. Feeling is a key component of manifestation, and is more powerful than it seems.

Wayne Dyer has a saying: "You get whatever you really, really, really, really want; however, you also get whatever you really, really, really, really don't want." An advantage of this approach is that the Source knows what you need better than you do, and can give you something better than you could have imagined. We will call this approach the Way of the High Priestess.

One thing to remember while working with manifestation is that if what you're asking for is not compatible with the beliefs of your subconscious mind, it will be a lot more difficult for you to make things happen. Hypnosis and repetition are two tools that can help.

Another thing to remember is that the subconscious mind draws conclusions about what you want based on your conscious thoughts and actions. For example, if someone believes that it is impossible to become rich without being ruthless and unethical, their subconscious mind would conclude that becoming rich is a bad thing if it requires being a bad person.

The contents of the subconscious mind are mostly formed during childhood, but, whatever your age today, it is still open to further input. Getting new beliefs and ideas into the subconscious as an adult is a bit harder than for children. On the other hand, even though a three-year-old can learn a new language without even trying, a twenty-three-year-old can still learn.

The key principles for getting new information into your subconscious mind are repetition and symbols. Hypnosis also works, and good ritual magic implicitly has hypnosis as a component.

Let's talk about repetition first. Chances are, you are already using repetition to program your subconscious mind. The problem is, you're doing it without realizing it. You're doing the programming if you complain about the same thing over and over. You're also doing it if, every time an idea comes up, you say: "I couldn't possibly do that." You're also doing it if you worry about a future event, or linger on a past event.

The answer is to use repetition about things that you want, and to stop repeating about things you don't want. Stop complaining: either fix it or let it go if you can't. Start thinking about what you want and how you'll feel when you get it.

The other tool for programming your subconscious is symbols. Symbols have the advantage of not being immediately recognizable, so there's not as likely to be resistance.

Part II

Strategy

Chapter 3

Introduction to Astrology

Astrology at its deepest level is the study of cycles and their interaction. The starting point is the natal or birth chart, which is a cross-section at the time of birth of all the cycles that we consider in astrology.

One cycle we experience on a daily basis is caused by the Earth rotating on its axis; as a result, the entire Zodiac appears to rotate around us once per day. Two important points in this cycle are the Ascendant and Midheaven, which you'll learn about below.

Another cycle takes place approximately once per month. The Moon starts off as a thin crescent, increases to a full circle, decreases to a thin crescent pointing the other way, and finally disappears entirely. This is the cycle of moon phases, and it plays a role both in your birth chart and going forward.

The third cycle involves the sun and the length of daylight. In the Northern Hemisphere, in late December the days are shortest and the nights longest; in late March the duration of daylight and night are equal; in late June the days are longest and the nights shortest; finally in late September the day and night are equal. This cycle is recorded in astrology as cycle of the Sun through the Zodiac.

These cycles take place against a background called the Zodiac, which is divided into twelve sections called signs. While there are constellations with the same names as the signs of the Zodiac, western astrology normally uses what is called the tropical Zodiac. Other astrology systems use the sidereal Zodiac, which is based on the actual constellations, but does not match them exactly.

The tropical Zodiac is defined starting with Aries, which starts with the Sun's position at the Spring Equinox. Similarly, Cancer starts with the Summer Solstice, Libra with the Autumn Equinox, and Capricorn with the Winter Solstice. There will be more detail about the Zodiac signs, along with the other elements of astrology, in the sections that follow.

3.1 Chart Points

We will begin by discussing some Zodiac points that are important in a chart: specifically, the Ascendant, Midheaven, Part of Fortune, and the Moon's Nodes. These points all have metaphorical meanings relating to the native's persona.

A^{sc} **Ascendant** The Ascendant is the point in the Zodiac that is on the Eastern horizon at the time of the chart. In a birth chart, it represents the personality of the native as seen by casual acquaintances. On a deeper level, it is the interface between the native and the world. For example, a native with a Scorpio Ascendant will not only have Scorpio qualities perceived by others, but will also look at the world with the eyes of a Scorpio.

D^{sc} **Descendant** The Descendant is the chart point directly across from the Ascendant, and it a metaphor for other people, specifically significant others.

♈︎ Midheaven The Midheaven is the point in the Zodiac that has the highest position in the sky at the time of the chart. It is thus a metaphor for the highest qualities the native should aspire to in life. As relates to personality, the Midheaven also determines how the native is perceived in public life.

IC The IC is the chart point directly across from the Midheaven, and is a metaphor for the native's inner life, including home and emotions.

⊗ Part of Fortune The Part of Fortune is an artificial chart point created from the positions of the Sun, Moon and Ascendant. Its position by sign and house indicates where and how the combined needs of identity, emotions and personality can be satisfied. Fulfilling these needs creates the precondition for good luck or fortune.

☊ North Node The nodes of the Moon are the points of the Zodiac where the Moon's orbit crosses the apparent orbit of the Sun (which is known as the Ecliptic). The North Node is the point where the Moon crosses the Ecliptic moving North. Its position by sign and house represent a direction of growth for the native.

☋ South Node The South Node is the point of the Zodiac where the Moon's orbit crosses the Ecliptic moving South. Its placement by sign and house represent a fallback position that the native may tend to rely on under stress at the expense of growth.

3.2 Houses

Charts in western astrology are typically drawn as circles divided into twelve sections, though this book uses a more traditional square chart, in which twelve smaller squares are arranged around a larger center square. These twelve sections are called houses, and the Zodiac is divided between them. The boundaries between the houses are called cusps. As an example, if the Second House cusp is 23 degrees into Sagittarius (in this book we'll write this as 23 ♐) and the Third House cusp is at 14 ♑, any planet between those two degrees would be in the Second House. There are various methods of defining these cusps; they are called house systems.

Most of the house systems use either the Ascendant, Midheaven, or both to determine the house cusps. The Placidus and Koch systems, for example, use the Ascendant as the First House cusp and the Midheaven as the Tenth House cusp. The rest of the cusps are then determined by taking a portion of the difference between them. The Whole Sign system, on the other hand, uses only the Ascendant to determine the house cusps. The First House cusp is the beginning of the sign in which the Ascendant falls. The Second house cusp is the beginning of the next sign, and so forth.

The Placidus system is the one most commonly used by western astrologers, but in this book we will be using the Whole Sign system. When working with your chart, you can use other house systems if you prefer, and you *should* use a different house system if the results make more sense to you. However, one of the planning techniques that will be given later was developed using the Whole Sign system; it will work using the other systems, but the math becomes a lot more complicated.

In keeping with the book's motto ("As above, so below."), the twelve houses correspond to twelve areas of our lives. What follows is not comprehensive (there have been entire books written about the Houses), but instead will serve as a starting point.

First House The First House was known as the Helm by the ancients, which means the place from which a ship was steered. It can best be thought of as our interface to the outside world, and contains the Ascendant, which is the primary determinant of personality. It also corresponds to the body.

Second House The Second House is about personal resources and values.

Third House The Third House is about our immediate environment. Other correspondences include brothers and sisters, trips short enough to return the same day, primary education, and communication.

Fourth House The Fourth House is about the home, emotions, and the father.

Fifth House The Fifth House is about things that come from inside you, children being the most prominent example. It can also refer to art and creative expression in general.

Sixth House The Sixth House is the house of Work. It covers day-to-day activities on the job or at home, but also your body's functioning, and people who work for you.

Seventh House The Seventh House is the house of the other. It covers people with whom you have important long-term relationships. The most common example is spouses, but you can also have long-time friends here, and long-time enemies.

Eighth House The Eighth House covers resources of others, like investments and debts. It also covers letting go of valued things.

Ninth House The Ninth House is a "Big Picture" type of place. It covers relgion and spirituality, also higher education and longer trips.

Tenth House The Tenth House covers career and reputation, as well as the mother; royalty in countries that have it, important people in any case.

Eleventh House The Eleventh House covers friendships, group activities and social causes.

Twelfth House The Twelfth House covers areas where you're "stuck," though it's traditionally the House of self-undoing, implying that if you're stuck, it's most likely your own fault. Other traditional attributions are prisons and enemies you don't know about.

3.3 The Planets

Traditional astrology used the five visible planets, but also counted the Sun and Moon as planets. Uranus, Neptune, and Pluto were unknown to the ancients, but were added to astrology soon after they were discovered[1]. The Planets correspond to parts of ourselves:

☉ **Sun** The Sun in astrology corresponds to basic identity and life purpose. The Sun rules Leo, so your life purpose will relate to whatever house is assigned to Leo, using resources associated with the house your sun is placed in.

☽ **Moon** The Moon corresponds to emotions and habits. The moon rules Cancer. The moon's placement will tell you where you will be able to meet your emotional needs. Doing that will facilitate activities of the house assigned to Cancer.

☿ **Mercury** Mercury corresponds to thought processes, communication and learning style. Mercury rules Gemini and Virgo. Mercury's sign and placement will tell you how to think, communicate and learn more effectively, which will facilitate activities of the houses assigned to Gemini and Virgo.

♀ **Venus** Venus attracts things and people of value. Venus rules Taurus and Libra. Venus' sign and placement will tell you how to attract nice things and people, which will facilitate activities of the houses assigned to Taurus and Libra.

---

[1] Some traditional astrologers question whether that was a wise thing to do.

♂ **Mars** Mars is your assertive force and energy, and rules Aries and Scorpio. Mars' sign and placement will tell you how to best go after what you want and deal with obstacles, which will facilitate activities of the houses assigned to Aries and Scorpio.

♃ **Jupiter** Jupiter corresponds to expansion and improvement, and rules Sagittarius and Pisces. Its sign and placement will tell you how you can best improve things and expand your horizons, which will facilitate activities of the houses assigned to Sagittarius and Pisces.

♄ **Saturn** Saturn corresponds to restriction, focus and selectivity, and rules Capricorn and Aquarius. Its sign and placement will indicate how and where you can focus your energies and be selective, which will facilitate activities of the houses assigned to Capricorn and Aquarius.

♅ **Uranus** Uranus breaks through boundaries, and can sometimes cause sudden or strange events. Modern astrology assigned rulership of Aquarius to Uranus, but my opinion is that Uranus, like Neptune and Pluto to follow, will operate wherever it needs to.

♆ **Neptune** Neptune is the great sea god, and dissolves boundaries. Neptune can provide inspiration and intuition, but also confusion and self-deception.

♇ **Pluto** Pluto transforms things in such a dramatic way that it can feel like death.

In real life, planets revolve around the Sun, but in astrology, everything is from our perspective here on Earth. As a result, the Planets (except for the Sun and Moon) do not continuously go forward through the Zodiac; each Planet will have at least one period per year where it appears to slow down, stop, go backward through the Zodiac, then stop and go forward again. The stops are called stations, and when a Planet appears to be moving backward, it is said to be Retrograde (℞).

3.4 Major Asteroids

Including some asteroids and Chiron to the birth chart can add some depth to the interpretation. This will be important to you if one of the items listed below occupies a prominent position in your chart. You should consider any of the items below if one of them:

- is in the 1st, 4th, 7th, or 10th house (referred to as angular).

- aspects the Sun or Moon by conjunction, opposition or square (more information on aspects to follow).

- aspects the Ascendant or Midheaven by conjunction or opposition.

⚷ **Chiron** Chiron is a comet that orbits the Sun between Saturn and Uranus. The name Chiron comes from a mythical centaur who was a healer and teacher. If Chiron is prominent in your chart, part of your mission might be healing or teaching.

⚳ **Ceres** The asteroid Ceres represents the Earth Mother goddess Ceres. If Ceres is prominent in your chart, so is your nurturing capacity.

⚵ **Juno** Juno is most famous in mythology for putting up with the philandering Jupiter. This asteroid represents your capacity for committing to a relationship and what you may need from that relationship.

⚴ **Pallas** The asteroid Pallas represents the goddess Athena/Minerva, the warrior goddess of wisdom. In your chart it represents wisdom that you find worth fighting for.

⚳ **Vesta** The asteroid Vesta represents the hearth goddess Vesta, as well as the Vestal Virgins, whose job it was to keep the temple flame lit at all times. Vesta in your chart represents where you may feel devoted to a cause.

3.5 The Signs

The Zodiac signs can be thought of as modes of operation for the Planets occupying those signs, but also determine the resources the Planets have to work with.

♈ **Aries** Aries is a Cardinal Fire sign ruled by Mars. As a Cardinal Fire sign, the emphasis is establishing personal identity and freedom, in an assertive manner because of the Mars rulership. Under stress, the Mars assertiveness can turn into aggressiveness or even violence.

♉ **Taurus** Taurus is a Fixed Earth sign ruled by Venus. As a Fixed Earth sign, the emphasis is on maintaining material security, but in style and comfort due to the influence of Venus. Under stress, the Fixed mode and Earth element can lead to obstinacy.

♊ **Gemini** Gemini is a Mutable Air sign ruled by Mercury. The emphasis here is on evaluating and distributing ideas, and promoting interaction and communication. Under stress, the combination can lead to flightiness.

♋ **Cancer** Cancer is a Cardinal Water sign ruled by the Moon. This sign has an emphasis on creating emotional security. Under stress, moodiness and clinginess are dangers.

♌ **Leo** Leo is a Fixed Fire sign ruled by the Sun. This sign has an emphasis on maintaining identity and freedom, and making sure everyone knows it. Under stress, there is a danger of becoming a "drama queen."

♍ **Virgo** Virgo is a Mutable Earth sign ruled by Mercury. This sign has an emphasis on evaluating physical things, and combined with the Mercury's emphasis on communication, accounts for Virgo's reputation as a nitpick.

♎ **Libra** Libra is a Cardinal Air sign ruled by Venus. This sign has an emphasis on creating communication and interaction, and making sure both are harmonious and graceful. Under stress, the danger is vacillation between denying one's needs in favor of harmony with others on one hand, and on the other hand, fighting over inconsequential slights in the name of justice.

♏ **Scorpio** Scorpio is a Fixed Water sign ruled by Mars. This sign has an emphasis on maintaining emotional security, with an assertive manner. Scorpio can be vindictive or passive-aggressive under stress.

♐ **Sagittarius** Sagittarius is a Mutable Fire sign ruled by Jupiter. This sign has an emphasis on evaluating and communicating about freedom and identity, with an emphasis on philosophy and expansion or horizons. Under stress, Sagittarius can be foolhardy or dogmatic.

♑ **Capricorn** Capricorn is a Cardinal Earth sign ruled by Saturn. This sign has an emphasis on creating material security and establishing structures. Under stress, Capricorn can seem aloof if not ruthless.

♒ **Aquarius** Aquarius is a Fixed Air sign ruled by Saturn. This sign has an emphasis on maintaining ideas and the structure thereof. Under stress, Aquarius can be controlling.

♓ **Pisces** Pisces is a Mutable Water sign ruled by Jupiter. This sign has an emphasis on evaluating emotions and looking at the "Big Picture." Under stress, Pisces tends to withdraw.

3.6 Aspects

An aspect is a relation between the position of two planets or other items in a chart. Some aspects are relatively harmonious; others are more stressful; some can be either depending on which planets are involved. What an aspect means is that the operations of the two planets are somehow related, for better or worse. This can be a good thing if you're aware of it, or a bad thing if not.

When determining if two planets are in aspect, we take the difference in position by degree and sign. Each sign has 30 degrees. This difference is compared to the exact distance of the aspect. If the difference is within a defined tolerance range called an orb, the planets are said to be in aspect.

As an example, let's say that Saturn is at 5 degrees of Aries, Venus at 2 degrees of Libra, and that we are using an orb of 5 degrees. There would be an exact opposition between the two planets if Venus were at 5 degrees of Libra, but since it is only 3 degrees away from that point, and the orb is 5 degrees, we count this as an aspect. If Venus were at 2 degrees of Leo, the aspect would be a trine instead of an opposition.

We will also be using what are called sign-based aspects, where we consider Planets to be in aspect if the first degrees of their respective signs are in aspect. Sign-based aspects are not as strong as degree-based aspects, but do have an effect. For example, if Venus is at 2 degrees of Libra, while Mars is at 16 degrees of Capricorn, the first degrees of their respective signs are 90 degrees apart, so there is a sign-based square between Venus and Mars.

There are at least ten aspects in common use today, but in this book we'll only be using the 5 classical aspects:

- ☌ **Conjunction** A conjunction is when two planets are in the same degree and sign, plus or minus the orb. It indicates that the two planets tend to operate together. Whether this is a good thing depends on the planets involved. Saturn conjunct Venus, for example, can indicate issues with relationships and money, or, under better circumstances, a person who is selective about the people and things in his or her life.

⚹ **Sextile** A sextile is when two planets are 60 degrees, or two signs, apart. It indicates a possibility for cooperation between the two planets. Mars sextile Moon, for example, could indicate a person who is comfortable being assertive when needed.

□ **Square** A square is when two planets are 90 degrees, or three signs, apart. It indicates that the planets are working at cross purposes and can be very stressful depending on the planets. Sun square Moon, for example, could indicate a person whose identity and emotions are in conflict, resulting in self-destructive behavior.

△ **Trine** A trine is when two planets are 120 degrees or four signs apart. It indicates a harmonious relationship between the two planets. Saturn trine Venus, for example, could indicate a person who has nice people in her life (a Venus function) because she has eliminated all of the undesirables and set strict boundaries (a Saturn function).

☍ **Opposition** An opposition is when two planets are 180 degrees or six signs apart. It indicates conflicting demands of the two planets, which will need to be balanced. Saturn opposite Venus, for example, could indicate a person who need for boundaries is perceived to work against the desire for nice companions. As a result, the person could let inappropriate people in his life and exclude suitable friends.

Missing from the list above are configurations where the planets are one sign apart or five signs apart. If two planets are exactly one sign, or 30 degrees, apart, the aspect is known as a semisextile (⚺). Five signs, or 150 degrees, apart, is a called a quincunx or inconjunct (⚻). These aspects are commonly used in modern astrology, but this book is based on traditional astrology and won't be using those aspects. Planets that are one or five signs apart do not share an Element or Mode, so they basically have nothing in common.

3.7 You're Every Sign!

The key lesson that astrology has to teach us is that none of us are one-dimensional; we each have every sign somewhere in our charts. As a result, we have the capacity to display qualities of every sign at some time or other in their lives. The qualities of each sign are more likely to appear in situations related to the house they occupy.

Gahl Sasson, in his book *Cosmic Navigator: Design Your Destiny with Astrology and Kabbalah* [4], recommends spending a month getting to know the qualities of each sign. I do like this approach, but a better way would be to practice New Moon Astrology [5]. Jan Spiller's book by that title recommends writing down intentions for the following month just after each New Moon. The book gives sample intentions that correspond to each sign. Following this program for a year will give you the opportunity to explore the qualities of each sign, and assess which qualities are lacking or could use improvement.

Chapter 6, which deals with yearly planning using what is called a Solar Return chart, lays out a planning method that will take you through one House and sign of your chart per year.

Chapter 4

Your Birth Chart

4.1 Obtaining Your Birth Chart

The first thing you'll need to obtain your birth chart is to find out when and where you were born, if you don't know already. The city, state and country should be enough for the where. For the when, an exact time is preferred. A birth chart can be done without the time, but the house information won't be available, and even the Moon position won't be precise enough for the techniques given in the next chapter.

Next, you'll need to decide on a house system. In my work, and in the examples given in this book, I use the Whole Sign house system, but you can use whatever system you like best. However, the techniques I will give later about planning the year ahead starting with your birthday will only work with Whole Sign houses.

Once that's done, you have a few options for having your chart computed, assuming you don't want to grab an ephemeris[1] and calculator.[2] There are a number of websites that will compute your

---

[1] a book listing the positions of the planets for each day
[2] Don't worry, you won't need an ephemeris...yet.

birth chart for free, but they may not have any flexibility for house systems. Another option is to buy or download a program to compute the chart for you. I prefer this option as the programs that are available will also be able to help with the techniques in the next chapter, which involve tracking the continued movement of the planets. Finally, you can hire a professional to compute and interpret your chart, and you should receive a copy of the chart as part of the deal.

Here's a sample chart. I'm using only the symbols for the planets and signs here. You can refer back to the descriptions in chapter 3. You may want to copy the symbols and items they refer to by hand on paper. That will help you commit them to memory.

4.2 Intepreting Your Chart

4.2.1 Personality and Life Purpose

Now that you have the chart, the first thing you want to look at is the Ascendant, or rising sign. The Ascendant determines your personality as seen by casual acquaintances. People who know you well will see your Sun sign characteristics more, and people who don't know you at all will see your Midheaven. You'll want to make sure the description fits. If it doesn't fit, it could be that your birth time is incorrect. This is important, because so many things on the chart depend on the Ascendant being correct.

Start with the description I gave in chapter 3 for your Ascendant. Now look for any planets in the First House. If you're using the Whole Sign house system, these planets will have the same sign as the Ascendant. These planets will modify your personality. For example, if you have Jupiter in your First House, you will have a more jovial (pardon the pun) personality. In the sample chart given, the Sun, Mercury and Neptune are all in the First House. Therefore you can expect the person belonging to this chart to be more charismatic and optimistic (the Sun), intellectual and talkative

(Mercury), and spiritual but prone to addiction (Neptune), all of which to a greater extent than you would expect of a Scorpio.

Next, look at the sign and house of the Ascendant's ruler. Scorpio is ruled by Mars, which is in Capricorn in the Third House. Since Mars is in Capricorn, that would lend a more practical, serious, and ambitious quality to the subject's personality. Mars being in the third house would make the subject more interested in communication, learning, and the immediate environment.

Finally, we will look at aspects to the Ascendant and the Ascendant's ruler. There's a sextile between the Ascendant and Mars, which happens to be the Ascendant's ruler. This is a good sign, but don't worry if you don't have that type of aspect in your chart. It just means that you won't be as easy for you to get your life on track. Sextiles aren't automatically fortunate anyway; they have to be activated by consciously seeking out the synergy between the two planets. In this case, the subject could activate the sextile by making a conscious effort to be more assertive (Mars energy applied to personality). There is also a sextile between the Ascendant and Pluto. The good news is that what I just wrote about needing to activate sextiles doesn't really apply to outer planets. The bad news is that normally this is because the outer planets take care of the activation for you, and as with all outer planet activity, your comfort won't be very high on the priority list when this happens.

Continuing with aspects, now let's look at aspects to Mars, the Ascendant ruler. There is a sextile from the Sun, and a trine from Pluto. This indicates Pluto will help by providing an impetus for transformation when needed and the necessary power. Since the Sun is in sextile, these changes will be in harmony with identity and life purpose once the proper groundwork has been laid.

Now we will repeat the process with the Midheaven. The Midheaven is the highest point of the Zodiac in the sky at the time of birth, and therefore analogous to the highest point in your psyche, and could even be interpreted as indicating a "calling." As part of your development, you will be exploring the qualities indicated by the Midheaven and working toward expressing them in your life.

We will start with the Zodiac sign of the Midheaven, which is Virgo. Virgo is a Earth sign, and therefore concerned with physical things. As a mutable sign, it is oriented toward evaluating and learning from what was started by the cardinal sign of the element and brought to completion by the fixed sign. Virgo has a reputation for being detail-oriented, and since ruled by Mercury, also for communicating about those details.

Unlike the Ascendant, which is by definition either the cusp (or boundary) of the first house, the Midheaven can have different locations using the Whole Sign house system, and can be in the tenth house, or the eleventh or ninth.

In the sample chart, the Midheaven is in the eleventh house. Therefore, the Virgo attention to detail should be applied toward group activities and social causes[3]. There are three other planets in the eleventh house with the Midheaven: Jupiter, Uranus and Pluto. Jupiter is the closest planet to the Midheaven, and is therefore known as "accidentally exalted," which just means that the planet indicates a special talent or gift. The presence of those three planets with the midheaven indicates that a calling might include enabling expansion and improvement (Jupiter) by helping people break out of limitations (Uranus) and transform their ways of thinking (Pluto).

Next, we look at the Midheaven ruler, in this case Mercury. Mercury is in Scorpio in the First House. The sign placement in Scorpio echoes the intensity and potential for transformation given by Pluto, and the First House placement indicates that this calling will be properly seen as part of the persona of the subject. He will be living his calling as much as performing it.

Now for aspects to the Midheaven and the Midheaven ruler. We've already discussed the conjunction between Jupiter and the Midheaven. There is also a sextile between the Midheaven and Mercury, the Midheaven ruler, as well as a sextile between Jupiter and

---

[3]like, for example, teaching people how to change their lives with Tarot and astrology

Mercury. This indicates that the benevolence and potential for improvement given by Jupiter can be used in furthering the goals given by the Midheaven.

The next element of the chart to examine is the Sun. The Sun indicates basic identity, but more importantly for this chapter, life purpose. Astrologer Demetra George [2] says that the life purpose is given by the house the Sun rules, and is accomplished using resources of the house where the Sun is placed. Let's apply this to the sample chart. The Sun rules Leo, which is the Tenth House in this chart. The Tenth House is about career, reputation, and public life. The resources given are from the Sun's placement in Scorpio in the First House. The placement indicates that resources will be the subject's personality, intensity and persistence.

Now let's look at aspects to the Sun. First, let's look at the conjunction with Neptune. Neptune can lend a spiritual component to the identity, or it can lend a tendency toward escapism or self-delusion. The subject will be well-served to cultivate his spirituality, as the alternative could well be escapism or addiction. There is also a conjunction with the Ascendant, which means that the subject views himself basically the same way he is viewed by others[4]. There are also two sextiles to Mars and Pluto. There is much power available in this configuration, and the calling indicated by the Midheaven would be a good outlet. We would normally at this point look at aspects to the Sun's ruler, but the Sun and Ascendant have the same ruler, so we're done with the Sun.

Next, we look at the Moon. The Moon rules emotional responses and habits, but also the body, which actually makes it the vehicle for carrying out the life purpose. The Moon is responsible for matters relating to whatever house has the sign Cancer, and uses the resources of the house where it's placed. In the sample chart, Cancer is in the Ninth House, and the Moon is in Pisces in the Fifth House. The Ninth House is about philosophy and higher education, among other things, and the Fifth House about creative expression. We

---

[4]to the extent that Neptune doesn't fog up everything

could say, then, about the sample chart, that the subject will implement his life purpose by using creative expression in the direction of philosophy and education, and that doing so will in the process satisfy emotional needs.

Now let's look at aspects to the Moon. Most prominent are oppositions to Uranus and Pluto. Remember that oppositions tend to be experienced as stress coming from others. In this case, the stress could come in the form of power struggles (Pluto) and could be sudden and be experienced as a desired to break out of what seems to be a confining situation (Uranus).

Finally, let's look at the Lot of Fortune and see how the subject can attract opportunities by acting from a place that harmonizes personality, identity and emotions. The Lot of Fortune is in Cancer in the Ninth House. The placement indicates that the subject can attract favorable opportunities in the areas of higher education and philosophy, by creating emotional security.

4.2.2 Relationships

Many of our problems in relationships are a result of improper choice of partners. Astrology can help with this by enabling us to identify what we need from relationships and what qualities we have to bring to relationships. There are also techniques of comparing and combining birth charts of the two people in a relationship in order to determine compatibility and potential trouble spots. In this book, we will focus on your needs and assume you'll find a suitable partner if necessary. We will be focusing on marriage in this section, but the information will also apply to any long-term romantic relationship.

The first thing to look at is the placement and condition of Venus, which represents the part of us that wants to have nice things and people in our lives. Creating and maintaining a healthy relationship is more difficult for some people than others, and the placement and condition of Venus will not only indicate any difficulties, but also tell us what to do about them.

We will also be looking at the Seventh House and its ruling

planet, the Seventh House being about significant relationships. Finally, there's a gender-specific planet to consider. For men, the sign and placement of the Moon give an indication of how they relate to their mothers, and by extension women in general. Conversely, for women the sign and placement of the Sun give an indication of how they relate to their fathers, and men in general.

In the sample chart, Venus is in Libra in the Twelfth House. This gives an indication of balance and harmony (Libra) as relationship needs, as well as karma (12th House). Venus is opposite Saturn in the birth chart. Since Saturn is about focus and structure, its opposition to Venus indicates that the subject may experience relationships as being restrictive. On the other hand, Saturn's placement in Aries indicates that the native should have whatever structure exists in his life organized around his identity and activities instead of the other way around. This of course implies that a traditional relationship may not work for the subject, at least not without a very careful choice of partner. This is actually echoed by a conjunction between Venus and Uranus, which indicates a need for some freedom and independence in the context of the relationship.

For this sample, Venus also happens to be the ruler of the Seventh House, and there are no planets in the Seventh House. If a different planet, say for example Mars, ruled the Seventh House, we would also look at the placement of Mars, and any planets aspecting it. In any case, we do need to look at the sign of the Seventh House, which is Taurus. The sign indicates that the subject will need some physical stability from the relationship.

Next, since the subject of the chart is male, we will look at the Moon's placement and aspects. We've already mentioned the Moon's oppositions from Uranus and Pluto, and the issues discussed above will also come out in dating and relationships.

4.2.3 Vocation

Another topic that astrologers are often asked about is career. Astrology can help by identifying what we need from our daily work and career in general. Career in astrology is governed by the Tenth House. Supporting information will also be provided by the Second and Sixth Houses, which are about resources and work habits respectively. The Midheaven is more related to vocation than career. If the Midheaven is not in the Tenth House, that would indicate that the career and vocation are more properly kept separate for that person.

The subject has Leo in the Tenth House, and the Sun as the Tenth House ruler. We can say, then, that the subject needs recognition and appreciation from his career, and he may have a tendency to identify himself with his career. In the sample, there are no planets in the Tenth House. If Mars, for example, were in the Tenth House, that would suggest a career where the subject could express assertiveness, and possibly something involving physical activity. If Mercury, on the other hand, were in the Tenth House, that would suggest a career involving communication of some sort.

The subject has Sagittarius in the Second House, and Jupiter as the Second House ruler, but no planets in the Second House. That suggests that the resources the subject can bring to the career include a sense of adventure (Sagittarius) and an ability to see the big picture (Jupiter). If Venus were in the Second House, for example, that would indicate that the ability to relate to others would be an important resource for the subject.

The subject has Aries in the Sixth House, with Mars as the Sixth House ruler, and Saturn in the Sixth House. With Aries in the Sixth House, the subject has a need to work independently, but also a need for structure in the work environment (Saturn). Since Mars, the Sixth House ruler, is placed in the Third House, communication is also important in getting daily work done.

4.3 Other Life Areas

The method given above for analyzing the Sun, Moon, Ascendant Ruler and Midheaven ruler should be applied to the rest of the planets in your chart. Doing this will help you become familiar with the rest of the facets of your psyche and thus learn the most important lesson of astrology.[5]

The general method is to analyze the sign and house placement of the planet to determine its mode and area of operation. The purpose of the planet's activities will be given by the house corresponding to the signs the planet rules.

In the sample chart, we've already had some discussion about Mercury as the Midheaven ruler, so let's look at the houses it rules: the Eighth and Eleventh. The Eighth House is about shared resources, including things we need to let go of, hence the association with death and beginnings and endings in general. The Eleventh House is about friendships and group activities. We could therefore say that the Mercury purpose in the sample chart is to get the native to play nicely and share his toys with others.

Similarly, we've had some discussion of Venus in association with relationship needs. As mentioned, Venus in the sample chart rules the Seventh and Twelfth House. The Seventh House is about relationships, and the Twelfth House about getting out of stuck places, among other things. So the Venus purpose for the sample native is getting above difficulties in relationships.

We've discussed Mars in the sample chart as the Ascendant ruler. Mars in the sample chart rules the First and Sixth houses. The First House is about personality and identity; the Sixth about daily work habits. So the Mars purpose for the native is defining identity and personality through daily work.

Now, let's look at Jupiter, which we've mentioned briefly in conjunction with the Midheaven[6]. Jupiter is about expansion and improvement, as well as the "big picture." Jupiter's not very well placed in Virgo, which is a very detail-oriented place. In the Eleventh House, the improvement and expansion comes in the context of group activities, with the Virgo mode of supplying the essential de-

---

[5] You have every sign in your chart.
[6] Pun intended.

tails that just make everything work. Jupiter rules the Second and Fifth Houses, so we can say that the Jupiter purpose is creative expression (Fifth House) using the native's resources (Second House).

Saturn in the sample chart is placed in Aries in the Sixth House. Aries is about establishing personal identity, and the Sixth House about daily work habits. The house and sign indicates that the native's need for structure is in the context of independent daily work. Saturn rules the Third and Fourth Houses, so the Saturn purpose for the native is communicating (Third House) with family in the home (Fourth House).

The analysis for Uranus, Neptune and Pluto will be less detailed, for two reasons. First, the planets move so slowly that the sign placement will be shared by everyone born within the span of a few years in the case of Uranus to a generation in the case of Pluto. The sign placement is important, but in a more "sign of the times" type of way. Also, I don't use the modern rulerships for these planets because my belief and experience is that the operate wherever they need to. So we'll just look briefly at the house placement.

The house placement of Uranus indicates where unexpected or sudden things can happen for the native (but not the only place), and areas of life where the native is more likely to feel restricted and attempt to break free. For the native, that area would be friendships and group activities because Uranus is in the Eleventh House.

The house placement of Neptune indicates where the native is more likely to be deceived or have illusions, or be prone to escapism. For the native, that area would be personality because Neptune is in the First House.

The house placement of Pluto indicates where the native might be prone to power struggles or have the capacity to be a transforming influence. For the native, that area would be friendships and group activities because Pluto is in the Eleventh House.

4.4 Development Planning

There are two things we will do with the information given by the birth chart. First, we will do what we can to correct any imbalances. Next, we will express the qualities of the Midheaven, which represents our highest goals.

A good starting point is a summary of strengths and weaknesses. We will use a concept called planetary condition to help with the list. Planetary condition will also tell us which planetary energies will be most likely to keep us on purpose, and which may be more likely to lead us off track. Planetary condition is basically a measure of how strong the energies of a planet are, and also how well these energies are oriented toward furthering your goals.

There are a number of factors to consider when evaluating the health of your planets. Let's start with the sign. A planet is more effective when it is in a sign that it rules, which is called the planet's domicile. For example, Jupiter is more effective in Sagittarius. Each planet has a sign besides its domicile(s) that is not quite as good as a domicile, but still good. A planet in that sign is said to be exalted. For example, the Moon is exalted in Taurus. The difference between a domicile planet and an exalted planet is analagous to the difference between being at home and visiting a good friend.

On the other side of the spectrum are planets in their detriment or fall. A planet is in its detriment when it is in a sign opposite to a sign it rules. For example, Jupiter would be in detriment in Gemini. Planets are not as healthy in detriment because they are in signs that have opposite qualities to their home signs. Jupiter is a "big picture" planet, for example, and Gemini is an immediate environment type of sign. A planet is in its fall when it is in a sign opposite to its exaltation. The Moon, for example, is in its fall in Scorpio. Continuing the analogy from the prior paragraph, a planet in fall is like having to stay at a cheap hotel instead of the friend's house. A planet in detriment is the same situation, but the room isn't quite clean.

The next thing to consider is the house a planet is in. Just as in real estate, certain locations are more favorable than others for doing business, and certain other locations are better for homes. We can divide the houses into three categories:

Angular The Angular houses are the First, Fourth, Seventh, and Tenth. They are called angular because in most house systems (but not Whole Sign houses) the angles (Ascendant and MC) and their opposite points (Descendant and IC) define the starting boundaries of these houses. Planets in angular houses, all other things being equal, are more effective at creating outward effects than planets in other houses.

Succeedent The Succedent houses are the Second, Fifth, Eighth, and Eleventh. They are called succedent because they follow the angular houses. Planets in angular houses are not quite as effective as planets in angular houses at producing outward effects.

Cadent The Cadent houses are the Third, Sixth, Ninth and Twelfth. Planets in cadent houses are least effective in producing outward effects, but most effective in changes under the surface.

The other thing about houses is that houses with some type of aspect relation, even a square or opposition to the First House are more directly oriented toward life goals and purpose. The houses with no aspect relation to the First House are the Second, Sixth, Eighth and Twelfth.

The next thing to talk about is what are called benefic and malefic planets. Traditionally, Venus and Jupiter have been thought of as helpful or "benefic" planets, while Mars and Saturn have been thought of as harmful or "malefic" planets. A more modern approach says that all planets are actually helpful in the long run, but their effects can be experienced as unpleasant. That's not very helpful to the person having to deal with a Venus-Saturn opposition in his birth chart. It's probably most reasonable to say that some planets can be challenging to deal with, but overcoming the challenge "builds character."

Also, even planets traditionally thought of as benefic can have harmful effect under stress. Consider, for example, a birth chart with the Sun squaring the Moon. This aspect would indicate that the native's identity and emotions tend to work at cross-purposes, leading her to do things contrary to her self-interest. However, squares are often projected out onto the outside world, so it can appear to the native as if bad things just seem to happen to her for no apparent reason.

We can simplify by saying that Mars and Saturn are necessary and helpful planets whose effects can be seen as unpleasant. Jupiter and Venus, on the other hand, have effects that are generally seen as pleasant, but are not always helpful.

4.4.1 Aspects

A conjunction between two planets indicates that their energies tend to operate at the same time. Whatever activates one will in some way also activate the other. Let's say as an example, that a native has Mercury conjunct Mars in his chart. In situations where he becomes angry, he may use words to express his anger. The problem is that he may not even realize he's doing that, which can lead to problems in his interactions with others. The answer is to be consciously aware of the link between the planets.

Trines are assets because they indicate that the planets involved operate together harmoniously, without any effort needed on the part of the native. It makes sense for the native to work to get into situations where this harmony would be useful. Someone with Mercury trine Jupiter, for example, would do well to seek a job where he would be communicating with rich and powerful people.

Sextiles are also assets, but take a bit of work on the native's part to become active. The native's task will be to recognize the common ground between the two planets and determine how it can best be used.

Squares and oppositions can be challenging, but the key is to recognize the potential for projection. Squares can be experienced as difficulties that seem to just happen; oppositions can be experienced as other people creating problems. In both cases the answer is to realize that your own attitude and thinking patterns can make a difference.

4.5 When to Seek Professional Help

Astrology is based on a number of simple concepts, but can become very complex when the concepts are combined. Also, it can be difficult to be objective about personal matters than can be brought up by chart interpretation. On the other hand, with the information in this book, you can get a basic sense of what needs to be worked on.

So what role does a professional have to play in this? First, if there has been a miscalculation, a professional will spot it quickly. Next, a professional can provide an objective, impartial viewpoint. If there are things that you know are problems but are still unsure how to resolve, the professional has most likely seen them before and will know what to do about it. Finally, doing astrology charts is a lot of work!

Figure 4.1: Sample Birth Chart

XI. ♍ MC 0:23 ♃ 3:25 ♀ 22:21 ☊ 27:58	X. ♌	IX. ♋ ⊗ 9:15	VIII. ♊
XII. ♎ ♀ 2:53 ☊ 26:37 ℞			VII. ♉
I. ♏ ☿ 1:45 ASC 18:29 ☉ 19:26 ♆ 23:55	Test Subject November 12, 1967 7:20 AM EST 83:29W 42:12N Natal Chart		VI. ♈ ♄ 6:17 ℞ ☊ 26:37 ℞
II. ♐	III. ♑ ♂ 15:14	IV. ♒	V. ♓ ⚷ 25:16 ℞ ☽ 28:40

49

50

Chapter 5

Transits and Progressions

In the last chapter, we talked about making a long-term plan for personal and spiritual development, based on the birth chart. However, certain types of changes are easier to make at certain times. This is because the birth chart is only a starting point.

The planets continue to move after you are born, and their current positions interact from time to time with positions in your birth chart. These interactions are called transits. The general effect of transits is an activation of the birth planet, which leads to activity in the areas of life indicated by the house or houses that planet rules. For example, if you have Taurus or Libra in your seventh house, it is ruled by Venus, so any current planetary activity interacting with Venus in your birth chart could indicate changes in your relationships.

Also, the birth chart positions advance at the rate of 1 day per year of life. These advanced positions are called progressions. The changes marked by progressions seem more to come from within, and new qualities arise that we didn't know we had.

We will be discussing both transits and progressions in this chapter.

5.1 Progressions

The basic idea behind progressions is that planetary activity in the first ninety days after birth mirrors internal changes that take place over the course of a lifetime.

The most important progression cycles are created by the Moon. In the ninety days following birth, the Moon will make three complete cycles through the Zodiac, and three lunation cycles (from New Moon through Full Moon and back). During each of the cycles through the Zodiac, the progressed Moon will make aspects to every planet in the natal chart, basically intensifying the activity of the affected planet for approximately two months.

The Sun and Ascendant will also change signs between two and three times. This will mark slight changes in identity and personality. Mercury, Venus and Mars will also change signs, marking changes in thought processes, interactions with others, and self-assertion. Sometimes progressions will affect even the outer planets if they switch from direct to retrograde or vice versa.

Let's look at a couple from the sample chart. On January 31, 2010, the progressed Moon was exactly opposite progressed Saturn. We can expect this progressed aspect to activate Saturnine energies in the native, and intensify the effects of any Saturn transits that may be taking place.

On October 24, 2010, the progressed Moon was conjunct the progressed Midheaven. We would expect the transit to mark an increased concern with career and vocation. In the life of the native, it coincided with the native starting to write a book.

5.2 Transits

Transits are the interactions that take place between the current planet positions, and the position of items in the birth chart, which can include the Ascendant and Midheaven. These interactions can have short-term, localized effects in the case of inner planet transits, or more pervasive, long-term effects in the case of outer planets (especially Pluto).

For the purposes of this section, we will only consider transits from Saturn, Uranus, Neptune and Pluto. Jupiter transits definitely count as long-term and can last as long as a few months if Jupiter goes retrograde during the period, but Jupiter influences are generally positive, and the only real danger is excess. Mars and the planets further in, including the Sun and Moon, have orbits that are too short for transits to last more than a couple of weeks. In that time frame, Tarot is a much more effective tool.

The other, more important, reason for concentrating on transits from Saturn, Uranus, Neptune and Pluto is that these transits often set the stage for major life changes. I would even go so far as to say that the correct response to an upcoming outer planet transit is to look for things that may need to change.

During a transit from Saturn, the areas of life ruled by the natal planet can be subject to a heightened degree of responsibility, and the atmosphere can feel restrictive. If the areas affected are places where you've been trying to get away with something, this will be the time to "pay the piper."

During a transit from Uranus, the affected areas will feel more restrictive, similar to a Saturn transit. The difference is that there will be pressure to "break out" of anything that feels restrictive. There is also the potential for very sudden change in any area that needs it.

During a transit from Neptune, there could be confusion or deception in the areas affected. Your challenge during these transits will be to see through the fog and achieve some clarity.

During a transit from Pluto, you may experience profound and pervasive changes in the areas of your life affected by the transit. You may be asked to change or to let go of something. The request will be polite at first, but it's not really a request. The areas affected will change despite your reluctance or your best efforts to the contrary.[1]

We will consider the same aspects for transits as we did for the natal chart:

- Conjunctions can be experienced as the natal planet taking on some of the character of the transiting planets. For example, if Saturn is transiting conjunct natal Venus, the native may feel more aloof in relationships and may prefer more austere surroundings.

- Sextiles can mark opportunities. For example, Uranus transiting sextile Mercury could indicate a sudden opportunity to break out of restrictions in the areas of the houses ruled by Mercury in the natal chart.

- Squares are often perceived as outside factors forcing a change. For example, Neptune transiting square natal Mars could mark a time when the native discovers the need to be more selective about getting into arguments, instead of getting upset over misunderstandings.

- Trines can be experienced as sudden progress or removal of barriers. As an example, Saturn transiting trine the Descendant could mark a re-evaluation of the native's significant relationships.

- Oppositions are commonly experienced through other people. For example, Uranus transiting opposite the Moon could be experienced as emotional instability caused by others.

Two things should be noted at this point. First, if you are tracking these transits for yourself, remember that all of this activity is

---

[1] Does it sound like I just went through one of those transits?

happening in your chart, so you have something to learn from it, even if it seems to be coming from other people or from factors beyond anyone's control. The other thing is that the planets don't really cause things to happen; think of them more as markers. In a holographic universe, what happens here is reflected in the stars.

A transiting planet is likely to have a noticeable effect whenever it is within two degrees of an exact aspect to the natal planet or chart point. As a result, the duration of the transit can vary from a few days (for a fast-moving Mars or Jupiter transit) to a few years (in the case of a Neptune or Pluto transit). The effects will be more intense the closer the transiting planet gets to an exact aspect. The exact aspect can happen once, but can be repeated three or even five times in the case where a planet has one or two retrograde periods around the aspect to the natal point.

Astrologer Bernadette Brady [1] has an excellent method of determining the effects of a transit. The natal house placements of both the transiting and natal planet determine the perceived cause of the outward activity. The current house placement of the transiting planet determines the agent of the outward activity, and the natal houses ruled by the planets the places changes by the outward activity. Brady has slightly different rules as to when the transit is active in the case of multiple hits due to the transiting planet having a retrograde period.

Let's try this method using a recent transit to the sample chart. Saturn made a conjunction to the natal Venus in the sample chart. The conjunction first went exact November 29, 2009, was exact again retrograde March 28, 2010, and exact the final time August 20, 2010.

The general nature of the event is that Venus and Saturn energies are combined, so the part of the native's psyche that wants to have nice things and people in his life would be modified by a Saturn-like restriction and structure. We can expect in this case that some of the nice things and people will go away. Saturn in his Father Time aspect is responsible for getting rid of things that have outlived their purpose.

To predict the possible cause of the event, we look at the natal placements of the planets involved. Saturn is in the Sixth House in the birth chart, and Venus in the Twelfth House. Brady says that the Twelfth House can be difficult because it includes repressed elements and can therefore have things come out in different areas. We can expect that the cause will come at least partially from something related to daily activities (Sixth House), but with contributing elements from any stuck areas (Twelfth House) and the houses that the stuck areas would correspond to if they were unstuck.

The area of operation of the event would be the house transiting Saturn was occupying during the transit, namely the Twelfth. The stuck areas would be expected to be prominent items during the transit.

The resulting effects of the transit would be most prominent in the houses ruled by both planets. Venus rules the Seventh and Twelfth Houses in the natal chart, and Saturn rules the Third and Fourth Houses. So we can expect limits and culling to take place in the areas of usual environment (Third House), home and emotions (Fourth House), relationships (Seventh House) and stuck areas (Twelfth House).

At the time of this writing, the transit has finished, so let's look at what happened in the life of the subject. At the time the transit started, the subject had a divorce pending, and had a mortgage on a house that was not worth as much as the mortgage. Between the time of the first exact transit and the second, the divorce was complete (Seventh House). Two days after the second exact transit, the subject moved into a rental house (Fourth House). One day before the third exact transit, the subject filed for bankruptcy. That last one doesn't seem to match, but there's a complicating factor that during the third exact transit, Pluto was also making an exact square by transit to Venus, not to mention that the Twelfth House can come out anywhere. As a result of the bankruptcy, a favorite restaurant was removed from the subject's usual environment. The divorce was finalized. There was a potential new relationship that the subject decided not to pursue because it would have been "settling." Also, the subject has a better idea of what he needs from a relationship, and embarked on a self-hypnosis program (definitely Twelfth House) to help with difficulties in creating healthy relationships.

I saved the analysis of the causes of the event for last, because sometimes that can be the most difficult part. One factor precipitating the divorce was that a co-worker (Sixth House) of the subject had an obviously better marriage. The other factor was a mental illness of the subject's then-spouse (Twelfth House).

58

Chapter 6

The Solar Return

If you've followed the suggestions of chapter 4, you now have a long-term plan for personal development. This plan may require periodic adjustments, and the solar return chart is a tool that can help. A Solar Return is when the Sun returns to the exact position in the Zodiac where it was in your birth chart. That will not always happen on your birthday, but will happen within 2 days of it.

How to get your Solar Return chart will depend on how you got your birth chart. If you downloaded or purchased software to compute your chart, the same software should be able to compute the date and time of the solar return. If it doesn't, you need new software that does. If you had your chart done by a professional astrologer, he or she should be able to do your Solar Return chart, for a fee of course. If you went to a website to get your birth chart, you'll probably want to download software to compute your Solar Return.

Your solar return chart will be used to help identity action items for the year ahead. Also, this would be a good time to determine upcoming transits and progressions that may require attention during the year ahead.

Figure 6.1: Sample Solar Return Chart

Item	Position	Natal House
☉	19 ♏ 26	1
☽	29 ♑ 57	3
☿	4 ♐ 23	2
♀	28 ♎ 39 ℞	12
♂	10 ♐ 36	2
♃	23 ♓ 34 ℞	5
♄	12 ♎ 41	12
♅	26 ♓ 55 ℞	5
♆	25 ♒ 55	4
♇	3 ♑ 39	3
⚷	26 ♒ 5	4
?	10 ♑ 28	3
⚳	14 ♐ 0	2
⚴	15 ♍ 52	11
⚵	18 ♏ 31	1
☊	4 ♑ 58 ℞	3
☋	4 ♋ 58 ℞	9
⊗	4 ♌ 49	10
Asc	24 ♉ 17	1
Mc	1 ♒ 39	4

6.1 Annual Profection

The first thing we will do with the solar return chart is identify a theme for the year ahead using a traditional technique called annual profection. This technique assigns a house for each year of life, starting with the First House. On your first birthday, the Second House becomes the theme, and so on, going back to the First House on your twelfth birthday.

The theme is given by the house in the rotation, and prospects for that theme are given by the placement and condition of the ruler of that house in the birth chart. We will also be looking at the profected house ruler's position in the solar return chart.

Transits and progressions involving the profected house ruler can be expected to have a greater impact than normal during the year ahead. As far as prospects for getting something accomplished relating to the theme, they are better if the house ruler is in an angular house in the birth chart and solar return chart.

Using our sample subject, let's analyze the year starting on his birthday, November 12, 2010. The subject will be 43 years old. The next lower multiple of 12 is 36, so we can simplify by subtracting 36 and adding 1, so that would make this an Eighth House year. Gemini is in the Eighth House in the birth chart, so Mercury would be the profected house ruler.

The first rule is that subjects that are indicated as comparatively easy in the birth chart will still be easy during the appropriate profection year, and more difficult subjects will still be difficult. For example, if your birth chart indicates relationship difficulties, even if your profection is a Seventh House year, relationships may still be difficult unless you've worked on the underlying issues.

With that in mind, let's take another look at Mercury in the birth chart. The sign placement in Scorpio is neutral, but it's strongly placed in the First House, and Mars, its sign ruler, is exalted in Capricorn in the Third House. From this we can infer that Mercury has a solid base of operation, and ample resources. In addition, there is a close sextile between Mercury and Jupiter. Jupiter is in the eleventh house which is succeedent, but very close to the Midheaven, so therefore also strong. We can conclude that prospects for the houses ruled by Mercury, the Eighth and Eleventh, are better than average.

Now we know that there are good prospects for Eighth House activities; the question is whether those things will be successful this year. Looking at the good points first, Mercury is in the profection house (Eighth) in the solar return, so it's right there in the place of activity. Also, since it's direct in motion, it will be able to provide tangible effects. There are a couple of unfavorable points. Mercury in Sagittarius in the return chart would be in the Second House of the birth chart, so not in relation to the birth Ascendant, and therefore may have a tendency to throw the subject off course. Also, Mercury is conjunct Mars in the return chart, so there may be a tendency for the subject to have decisions clouded by anger.

One of the most prominent outer planet transits to Mercury in the year starting with the 2010 Solar Return is a trine from Chiron starting in February 2011, and ending in December 2011. Chiron represents the "Wounded Healer" archetype, and Mercury is about communication and learning. Brady has trine transits normally indicate an acceleration of the activity corresponding to the planet combination; the acceleration is due to the sudden removal of obstacles. The expected event will have something to do with communication, learning, and healing, and the removal of a related obstacle, causing rapid progress.

Chiron is in the Fifth House in the natal chart, and Mercury in the First, so the expected cause of the event will have something to do with creative expression and the personality of the subject. The field of operation will also be creative expression, and the results will be in the areas of shared resources (including debts) and group activities and friendships.

6.2 Yearly Progressions

As part of the yearly planning it's a good idea to also examine transits and progressions for the year ahead. Let's start with progressions. Progressions will mark significant internal changes in the native, and therefore intensify the effects of any transits involving the same planets as the progressed aspect.

Pluto, a marker of major transformation, will make a square to the progressed Ascendant in March 2011 and turn retrograde in April 2011. We can expect the subject to experience a major shift in self-image around this time period.

Another interesting event is the progressed Moon entering Scor-

Figure 6.2: Sample Progressions 2010-2011

Date	Progressed Planet/Sign	Aspect	Affected Point
12/25/2010	☽ ♎	△	progressed ♂
1/29/2011	☽ ♎	☌	natal ⚷
3/8/2011	♇ ♍	□	progressed ASC
3/31/2011	☉ ♑	△	natal ♃
4/7/2011	♇ ♍	Station Retrograde	
4/20/2011	☽ ♎	✶	progressed ASC
4/24/2011	☿ ♑	✶	natal ☿
5/25/2011	☽ ♎		progressed ☊
7/23/2011	☽ ♎		natal ☊
10/17/2011	☽ ♎	Enters ♏	

pio in October 2011, and therefore the subject's natal First House. Since the First House is the native's "window on the world," the progressed Moon there will cause more attention to the native's public life.

6.3 Yearly Transits

We've already discussed how to determine what the possible effects of a transit will be, and we will use this to help plan the year's activities. The idea is that some of the transits will strongly encourage, if not force, changes to be made. If we can identify these changes and make them willingly, we will be ahead of the game.

Figure 6.3 lists transits for the year beginning with the day of the 2010 Solar Return. Only the outer planets and Chiron are included in the transiting planet. The date listed is the date the transit becomes exact. You may notice that some of the transits occur multiple times. This is a normal result of the outer planets having one retrograde period per year, and a transiting outer planet can have an exact hit on the natal planet up to five times.

This seems like a lot of information to cover, even for a whole year. However, some of these transits will be more important than others. Bernadette Brady gives some simple rules for this:

1. The slower the transiting planet moves, the more important the transit will be. For example, transits from Pluto will be more important than transits from Mars.

2. The faster the natal planet or point moves, the more important the transit will be. This means that transits to the Sun, Moon, or Ascendant will be much more important than transits to Mars or Saturn.

3. Divide the number of signs (1 for conjunction) between the two planets into 360. The higher the number, the more important the transit will be. For example, a conjunction is more important than a trine, other things being equal.

If you generated the solar return chart on your computer, the software may also be able to rank the transits in intensity according to the rules above. If not, you can still use the guidelines above. Don't worry about ranking them exactly; the important thing is that you don't miss anything important.

That said, the Neptune transiting opposition to the Midheaven seems to demand the most attention. As mentioned in Chapter 3, Neptune dissolves boundaries. This can be an uncomfortable process, as we tend to think we need those boundaries, especially in the contexts of home and career, which are the significations of the two chart points affected by this transit. This process can first appear as confusion, and can be expected to start some time around April 2011, and to last through the end of 2012. We can expect a career change to take place at some point during the operation of the transit, but it won't be a change the subject will have much control over. Since Neptune is in the First House in the birth chart, we can expect concern with identity (or possibly health) to be a driving factor, as well as creative endeavors as Neptune is transiting through the Fifth House.

The next transit we will want to look at is an transiting Uranus opposite Venus in the birth chart. In general Venus is responsible for having nice things and people in the native's life, and that responsibility is emphasized by the fact that Venus rules the Seventh House in the sample chart. One of the effects of Uranus transit activity is the destruction of obstacles and restrictions. Putting all of this together, we can expect a potential love interest to appear on the scene in early May 2011, just in time for the career confusion and possible career change from the last paragraph. The transit activity is expected to continue until early 2012.

Figure 6.3: Sample Transits 2010-2011

Date	Transiting Planet/Sign	Aspect	Natal Point
12/9/2010	♄ ♎	□	♂
1/10/2011	♃ ♓	☍	♅
1/14/2011	♃ ♓	☌	☽
1/29/2011	♇ ♑	□	♄
1/30/2011	♅ ♓	☍	♅
2/6/2011	♃ ♈	☍	♀
2/8/2011	⚷ ♓	☍	MC
2/15/2011	♅ ♓	☌	☽
2/22/2011	♃ ♈	☌	♄
2/28/2011	⚷ ♓	△	☿
3/15/2011	♄ ♎	□	♂
3/26/2011	⚷ ♓	☍	♃
4/1/2011	♃ ♈	□	♂
4/19/2011	♆ ♓	☍	MC
5/3/2011	♅ ♈	☍	♀
5/19/2011	♃ ♈	☌	♌
6/6/2011	♃ ♉	△	MC
6/13/2011	♃ ♉	☍	☿
6/22/2011	♃ ♉	△	♃
6/23/2011	♇ ♑	□	♄
7/19/2011	♆ ♓	☍	MC
8/27/2011	⚷ ♓	☍	♃
9/1/2011	♄ ♎	□	♂
9/18/2011	♅ ♈	☍	♀
10/4/2011	⚷ ♓	△	☿
11/10/2011	♃ ♉	△	♃

Part III

Tactics

Chapter 7

Introduction to Tarot

Tarot is one of the two major tools you will use for the Great Work. We will be discussing how to use Tarot for tactical planning, which is addressed toward short-term goals. Tactical planning answers two questions: "What do I most need to examine or address at this point in time?" and "What's a good way to address this issue?"

    A Tarot deck is normally composed of 78 cards. Some decks may have more or less, but for use with this book, you'll want one with 78 cards. Decks are available in a wide variety of designs. There's most likely a deck with any theme you would be interested in, whether it be witches, nature, vampires, clowns, even cats. The deck to choose is one you like and are comfortable with. Some stores have demo decks you can look through, and there are also websites that have sample pictures for each deck.

    The standard Tarot deck is organized into two sections called the Major Arcana and the Minor Arcana. "Arcana" is the plural of the Latin word *arcanum*, which can be translated as "secret."

    However, I'm not sure "secret" is the right term for Tarot cards. There may be some secrets hidden in the designs of the cards originally, but there is still value in using the cards even if you don't know the meanings of all of the symbols. As mentioned above, the designs of the decks vary so much that they all have their own symbols anyway. Also, a lot of the meaningful aspects, especially in the Rider-Waite deck, are more hidden in plain sight than kept secret. Take the Death card for example: the picture shows the Grim Reaper on a horse, with a dead king in front of him, a priest with his head bowed in prayer, and two other people looking away. A child in the foreground kneels and offers Death a flower. An obvious message is that only the religious or spiritual, and the childlike or innocent, are capable of facing Death.

The Major Arcana has twenty-two cards. Each of the cards has a name and (with the possible exception of The Fool) a number. In readings these cards tend to indicate major if not karmic issues or stages of development. These cards can also be looked at as stages of growth in a process known as "The Fool's Journey." In this journey, the Fool represents a traveler who learns a lesson from each of the other Major Arcana cards. If you would like to learn more about the Fool's Journey, some of the Tarot books listed in the bibliography will have more details.

The Minor Arcana has fifty-six cards. These cards are organized into four suits, one for each of the Four Elements. Each suit has an Ace, a set of four Court Cards, and cards numbered Two through Ten. The Court Cards are the King, Queen, Knight and Page. With some decks, the King will be called a Prince, or the Page may be called a Knave or even a Princess. The Court Cards can often represent people, but if they don't, they will represent qualities that the people would have. The numbered cards generally represent events and our reactions to them.

Tarot is primarily a symbol system, and more generally, a tool. Like any tool, it can be used for many purposes and works more efficiently for some purposes than others. As a symbol system, Tarot has a rich heritage going back at least to the Middle Ages if not further. There are associations with astrology, qabalah, and alchemy.

There seems to be an association between Tarot and devil worship in the minds of some people who don't know much about either, and are obviously just going by whatever they've heard or seen in movies. That's not to say that there's no association: I'm sure Tarot can be used to help summon evil spirits, in the same way that a screwdriver can be used to pound nails or cut wood. You may wonder who in their right mind would do that with a screwdriver. The answer is someone who doesn't know what a screwdriver should be used for and who also doesn't know the best tools for pounding nails and cutting wood.

Also, we won't be discussing any tall, dark strangers. That sort of thing is fortune-telling. There's nothing wrong with fortune-telling, but it's not the focus of this book. What we'll be doing is more properly referred to as *divination*, or accessing the contents of our subconscious minds, and connecting to the Source.

We will be using Tarot for brainstorming, and for tactical planning. The ideal use of Tarot is to have a question in mind, and draw random cards in a suitable layout. The interpretations of the cards drawn should supply food for thought about the question. Tarot, used properly, doesn't give the answer as much as supply better questions.

Chapter 8

The Minor Arcana

8.1 Overview of the System

The Minor Arcana cards are organized into four suits, which correspond to the four elements. Each suit has a set of four court cards, an Ace, and cards numbered two through ten.

Traditionally, the court cards represent people. Kings would represent older men, Knights younger men, Queens women of any age, and Pages children. Some readers still use the traditional meanings, but most use a more modern interpretation in which the cards correspond to people with characteristics given by the suit and title of the card. As a result, the Queen could be taken to refer to a man, and women can be Kings or Knights. A Knight is as a Knight does. The table that follows will show you how to derive those characteristics. The number cards represent events or emotions. For example, the Five of Cups is commonly interpreted to mean grief or regret. These meanings can also be derived, but more information is required. To interpret the number cards, we need a Planet, Sign, and Number, as shown in Table 8.1.

Pages Pages are assigned all three signs of the Element matching

Table 8.1: The Decans

Sign	First Decan	Second Decan	Third Decan
Aries	Mars	Sun	Venus
Taurus	Mercury	Moon	Saturn
Gemini	Jupiter	Mars	Sun
Cancer	Venus	Mercury	Moon
Leo	Saturn	Jupiter	Mars
Virgo	Sun	Venus	Mercury
Libra	Moon	Saturn	Jupiter
Scorpio	Mars	Sun	Venus
Sagittarius	Mercury	Moon	Saturn
Capricorn	Jupiter	Mars	Sun
Aquarius	Venus	Mercury	Moon
Pisces	Saturn	Jupiter	Mars

their suit.

Queens Queens are assigned the cardinal sign of the Element matching their suit.

Kings Kings are assigned the fixed sign of the Element matching their suit.

Knights Knights are assigned the mutable sign of the Element matching their suit.

Aces Aces are assigned all three signs of the Element matching their suit.

Twos, Threes, Fours Twos, Threes and Fours are assigned the cardinal sign of the Element matching their suit. Twos are assigned the planet ruling the first decan of that sign; Threes the planet of the second decan; Fours the third.

Fives, Sixes, Sevens Fives, Sixes and Sevens are assigned the fixed sign of the Element matching their suit. Fives are assigned the planet ruling the first decan of that sign; Sixes the planet of the second decan; Sevens the third.

Eights, Nines, Tens Eights, Nines and Tens are assigned the mutable sign of the Element matching their suit. Eights are assigned the planet ruling the first decan of that sign; Nines the planet of the second decan; Tens the third.

My interpretations of the Minor Arcana will be primarily derived from the astrological attributions given above. Of course, as you become familiar with the cards you will develop your own personal interpretations. This is a good thing.

In summary, the Court Cards represent roles or actors, the Ace is the theatre, and the number cards scenes.

8.2 Wands

We will start with an initial interpretation of all Wands as being about the quest for freedom and realization of identity.

Page of Wands The Page of Wands is learning about freedom and identity, and all aspects of the issues associated with them. Pages are also associated with messages, so the card could indicate a message about freedom, identity or initiative.

Queen of Wands The Queen of Wands corresponds to the Zodiac Sign Aries, which is a Cardinal Fire Sign ruled by Mars. She is beginning (Cardinal) to define and assert (Mars) her identity (Fire). A more traditional interpretation of the Queen of Wands is a witty, outgoing person. Queens can be mothers, and the Queen of Wands' response to a child with a scraped knee might be to tell the child to be brave, which in theory would make the knee not hurt so much.

King of Wands The King of Wands corresponds to the Zodiac Sign Leo, which is a Fixed Fire Sign ruled by the Sun. He maintains (Fixed) his identity (Sun, Fire) and freedom (Fire), while serving as a light (Sun) to his people. The King of Wands doesn't talk to people; he grants audiences.

Knight of Wands The Knight of Wands corresponds to the Zodiac Sign Sagittarius, which is a Mutable Fire Sign ruled by Jupiter. He evaluates (Mutable) freedom and identity issues (Fire), and loves to go on quests (Jupiter), but loves showing off (Fire) even more.

Ace of Wands All Aces represent beginnings, and this Ace represents initiative, and by implication, opportunity. The Ace of Wands is the fire that Prometheus stole from the gods. If you see this card, that fire is active in your life as well. Make good use of it.

Two of Wands The Two of Wands is Mars in Aries. Twos can mean alternation or decision. Mars is self-assertion and Aries about establishing identity and freedom. Putting all of the above together, the card indicates a decision about identity, and a willingness to fight for that identity if necessary.

The standard image for the card shows a man outside on a castle wall, holding a globe and looking out over the landscape. The figure of speech "He's got the whole world in his hands" comes to mind. If you see this card in a reading, you should ask yourself where you have the opportunity to make a decision about how to proceed.

Three of Wands The Three of Wands is Sun in Aries. Threes indicate growth and multiplication, the Sun identity, and Aries establishing identity and freedom. In combination, we can say that the card indicates progress along the path decided in the Two of Wands above.

Let's compare that to the standard image, which shows a man standing on a shore looking out over the sea. There are boats sailing in the distance. This card also has a catch phrase: "Waiting for his ship to come in." If you see this card in a reading, take the opportunity to assess your progress in something you may be currently working on. The answer may surprise you.

Four of Wands The Four of Wands is Venus in Aries. Fours indicate stability; we've already talked about Aries, and Venus is the planet of nice things and people. Putting them together, we can interpret the card as saying it's time to take advantage of the stable situation and do something involving nice things and people.

The picture on the card reflects that. The four wands hold up a canopy in the village square, and it's obvious from the picture that preparations are being made for some sort of celebration or festival. If you see this card, ask yourself if there's something you've been working on that it's time to take a break and assess what you've done. Champagne may be in order; just don't overdo it (see the next card).

Five of Wands The Five of Wands is Saturn in Leo. Fives are about destabilization, Saturn about structure and focus, and Leo about maintaining freedom and identity. The combination is stressful, and can mean competition or practice.

The standard picture on this card is of five young people sparring with staffs. Each one seems to just be trying to hit whoever he can while avoiding being hit himself. This card may be prompting you to ask where you need to prove yourself; not necessarily involving a fight (that's the Five of Swords), but instead to establish yourself as someone to be taken seriously.

Six of Wands The Six of Wands is Jupiter in Leo. Sixes are about balance and harmony, Jupiter about expansion and improvement, and Leo about maintaining freedom and identity. The traditional intepretation of the card is victory.

The standard picture is of a man on a horse in a victory procession. Everyone is cheering him on as he parades through the village square. This card may be asking if you can be a gracious winner and accept the accolades without getting a big head about it.

Seven of Wands The Seven of Wands is Mars in Leo. Sevens are about multiplication of concepts, Mars about assertion. The traditional meaning is standing up for yourself against everyone else.

The standard picture is of a man standing on a hill brandishing a wand. Six other wands point up at him from below. He's ready to battle the crowd, but his shoes don't even match. So if you see this card, make sure your shoes match before you decide to fight the world. Sometimes when you think everyone else is wrong, it's not everyone else.

Eight of Wands The Eight of Wands is Mercury in Sagittarius. Eights are about consolidation, Mercury communication and learning, and Sagittarius about evaluating identity and freedom. The traditional meaning is quick action or news.

The standard picture is of eight staffs flying through the air. If you see this card, something is going to happen soon, so get ready.

Nine of Wands The Nine of Wands is the Moon in Sagittarius. Nines are about completion, and the Moon about emotions and habits. Completion of evaluating identity and freedom can be a good thing, but the effects on the emotions can be mixed. One traditional meaning of the card is "battle-tested."

The standard picture shows a grizzled guard holding a wand in front of a fence formed by the other eight. If you see this card in a reading, you should ask if you really still need to keep your guard up.

Ten of Wands The Ten of Wands is Saturn in Sagittarius. Tens are beginnings, but based on something recently completed. With Saturn in Sagittarius, the completion could be of taking on responsibilities, and too many of them based on Jupiter's rulership of Sagittarius. That's also the traditional meaning.

The standard picture is of a man carrying ten wands at once, and looking at the picture it is not really clear how he can manage the feat. If you see the card, you should ask yourself if you've taken on more than you can comfortably handle.

8.3 Cups

Page of Cups The Page of Cups is learning about emotions, or could be someone about to start a new relationship. Pages can also denote messages, so there could be a message about an emotional matter.

Queen of Cups The Queen of Cups, as a Cancer, is all about making herself and others feel safe; in other words, establishing (Cardinal) emotional security (Water). She wants you to know that everything will be all right, and that you have nothing to worry about.

King of Cups The King of Cups is a Scorpio: Fixed Water, or in our system, maintaining emotional security, but ruled by Mars, so uses assertiveness to maintain that security. When things are good, anyway. As a Scorpio, the King of Cups may seem aloof and uncaring on the surface, but consider a contemporary symbol for Scorpio: the iceberg. Only 10 percent of the iceberg is above water; the rest is below the surface and unseen.

Knight of Cups The Knight of Cups is a Pisces: Mutable Water, or evaluating and distributing emotional security, under the

Jupiter influence of expansion and improvement. He is prone to going on quests and taking up causes. He probably needs to spend some time taking care of himself instead of saving damsels in distress all the time.

Ace of Cups Aces signify beginnings, and the Ace of Cups signifies emotional beginnings. The Ace of Cups is a very big cup in real life: the ocean of the collective unconscious. There's something for you in there of an emotional nature. Maybe it's a new relationship. Maybe it's a better understanding of someone who is already a part of your life. In any case, if this card shows up in a reading, cast out a line and see what you can reel in.

Two of Cups The Two of Cups is Venus is Cancer. Cancer in our system means establishing emotional security. One obvious meaning of Two is relationship, and this is emphasized by the Venus influence.

The picture on the card is of a young man and woman meeting to share a drink. Their arms interlock as they hold up their cups, and a caduceus with a lion's head grows from between the cups. One traditional meaning of the card is a connection. If you see this card, you can look at it as an opportunity to establish a new connection or fix an existing relationship.

Three of Cups The Three of Cups is Mercury in Cancer. Threes signify growth and expansion, and Mercury communication. The combination indicates the growth and expansion of an emotional relationship through communication, which is pretty close to the traditional meanings of friendship and celebration.

The standard picture is of three young women holding cups and dancing in a circle. If you see the card, you can ask what or who you might want to re-connect with.

Four of Cups The Four of Cups is the Moon in Cancer. Fours denote stability, and the other two factors are strictly emotional.

Cancer is the Moon's home sign, and the Four of Cups can show a tendency to become complacent.

The picture is of a young man sitting under a tree, seemingly in deep thought, or in the alternative, general apathy. Three cups are lined up in front of him, and he doesn't notice a fourth cup being offered to him from a little cloud. This card may be asking if there's an area of your life where you've become complacent.

Five of Cups The Five of Cups is Mars in Scorpio. Fives are about adjustment, and Scorpio about maintaining emotional security. Also, Mars is more comfortable making people adjust than doing the adjusting. Traditional meanings of the card include disappointment and regret.

The card shows a man in a cloak moping and looking down at three spilled cups in front of him. Two more upright cups are behind him. If you see this card, and you've recently experienced a disappointing situation, you should ask if there's a bright spot or silver lining.

Six of Cups The Six of Cups is the Sun in Scorpio. Sixes are about balance and harmony, and the Sun about identity. Combine the two with sustained emotional security, and you get the picture on the card: A little boy offers a cup with flowers planted in it to a little girl next to him. The two are outside in the village square by themselves.

Traditional meanings of this card include safety and nostalgia. This card does say that you're in a happy, safe place, but do you really belong there, or are you trying to hold on to the past?

Seven of Cups The Seven of Cups is Venus in Scorpio. Venus is the planet of nice things and people, and seven is about multiplication of abstract concepts. Put them together and one result is thinking about nice things and people; in short, daydreaming. A complicating factor is that Venus is not well placed in Scorpio and has a tendency toward unsuitable fixations there.

The picture on the cards echoes this meaning. A man is looking at seven cups in the background. The cups emerge from a curtain of cloud and each cup contains something different; for example, one contains a dragon, another a tower.

Eight of Cups The Eight of Cups is Saturn in Pisces. Eights are about consolidation of the new activity of Seven. Pisces in our system is evaluating emotional security. By the way, Saturn is the loneliest of the visible planets, which leads to the traditional meaning and picture. The traditional meaning is leaving a situation behind in search of something better. The picture is of a man leaving a group of eight cups and hiking toward a mountain in the distance. If you see this card in a reading, you should ask if there's a situation you want to leave behind in order to find something better.

Nine of Cups The Nine of Cups is Jupiter in Pisces. Nines are about completion, Jupiter about expansion and improvement, and Pisces translates into evaluating emotional security. Pisces is one of Jupiter's home signs, and the combination seems complacent.

The traditional meaning of the card is individual gratification. The picture is of a wealthy man standing with his arms crossed and a smug smile on his face. This card could be telling you that it's O.K. to have a good time, but you should include others in the fun as well.

Ten of Cups The Ten of Cups is Mars in Pisces. Tens are new beginnings based on the ending given by Nine. Mars adds initiative and action to what could be the ultimate in saccharine happy endings.

The traditional meaning is shared happiness. The picture is of a happy family under a rainbow of ten cups. If you see this card, it could be saying that even though the story has a happy ending, the "happily ever after" part is up to you.

8.4 Swords

Page of Swords The Page is learning about Air topics, such as thought processes, communication, truth and justice.

Queen of Swords The Queen of Swords, as a Libra, wants balance and harmony. Most of the time. Unless she wants justice instead. In any case, she won't be amused by any funny business you may have, so don't even try.

King of Swords The King of Swords, as an Aquarius, already has truth and justice established. Things may not seem right and true from your perspective, but there's only one opinion that counts in the matter, and it's not yours.

Knight of Swords The Knight of Swords, as a Gemini, is off and running, currently spreading the truth and justice the King has established, but that could change in a few minutes. A little exercise does a body good in any case.

Ace of Swords Like the other Aces, this Ace is about beginnings. The beginning could be in the direction of clarity about an issue, or it could be about setting right an injustice. If you see this card, it's time for you to gather the information you need and make a stand based on it.

Two of Swords The Two Swords is assigned the Moon in Libra. The Moon symbolizes emotions and habits, Twos are about alternation and duality, and Libra about establishing thought and communication. The combination indicates trouble deciding how to feel or what to say about a situation.

The traditional picture shows a young woman in a dress sitting on a stone block, blindfolded, holding two swords in arms folded across her chest. The posture and blindfold say "Leave me alone. I don't want to talk about it." If you see this card in a reading, know that even though you need some time to think, you'll have to take off the blindfold sooner or later.

Three of Swords Saturn in Libra. Threes are growth and expansion, and Saturn's exalted in Libra, but the standard picture shows a heart pierced by three swords. What's going on here? Well, Three's more of a Jupiter kind of thing, and the only thing Saturn really knows how to multiply are fears and restrictions.

One thing to note about this card is that the sword-pierced heart in the traditional picture is two-dimensional. The other thing to notice is the rain in the background. The two taken together say that whatever painful event is going on is necessary to clean up something, and that there's no lasting harm underneath.

Four of Swords Jupiter in Libra: Fours represent stability, while Jupiter represents expansion and improvement, but also faith.

This card could be saying that the apparent lack of activity is only temporary, and is a necessary preparation for bigger and better things.

Five of Swords Venus in Aquarius, combined with the Adjustment of Five. Venus doesn't mind adjustment, but Aquarius as a fixed sign is not so amenable. The traditional picture shows an obvious winner, and obvious losers in the background, so someone will have to adjust whether they like it or not. And my money's on "not."

The traditional meaning of the card is a clear victory or defeat, but it might be more useful to think of it as a forced adjustment. If you having to make an adjustment is outside of your control, at least you may be able to make the adjustment on your own terms. So if you see this card, you may want to ask if there are any areas of your life where you may be in denial about a need for change.

Six of Swords Mercury in Aquarius, combined with the balance and harmony of Six. Mercury doesn't do fixed signs well, but the balance of Six makes up for that. The Six of Swords is a good representation of what happens when you handle a Five of Swords situation correctly.

This card may be telling you that it's time to move on from something in your life that's been more stressful than necessary.

Seven of Swords Moon in Aquarius, combined with Seven's generation of new ideas. As a Fixed Air sign ruled by Saturn, Aquarius can have strongly held opinions about how things should be structured. Under stress, subjects of this influence are prone to give up on the group and go off to do things their way.

If you see this card, you should ask if there's something that bothers you about the procedures or rules you have to live under. Realize that even though it seems tempting to shortcut or ignore established processes, there's risk involved. Maybe talking with someone about it–and listening to what they have to say–will be a better solution.

Eight of Swords Jupiter in Gemini, combined with the stability of Eight. Jupiter is not well placed in Gemini–it's a "big picture" planet in a detail-oriented sign–and as a result the stability is not of a favorable kind. The expansion and improvement that Jupiter wants is blocked by Eight's stability in spite of the Gemini efforts to spread the word. "Unfavorable stability" could also be expressed as "self-imposed bondage," which is the traditional meaning given to the card.

This card tells you that if you are in a confining situation, the bonds are of your own making. Specifically, they may be the result of your thoughts or beliefs. Or maybe you should really have talked to someone instead of shortcutting the process (see the Seven).

Nine of Swords Mars in Gemini, combined with the completion of Nine. Completion is good, but Mars in Gemini not so much. A violent planet in a thought and communication sign may mean that it's regret and fear that are complete.

If you see this card, remember that even if you're in a bad situation, regret, fear and worry won't improve anything.

Ten of Swords Sun in Gemini, combined with the new cycle based on the completion of the old signified by Ten. The new cycle is based on communication (Gemini) of identity and purpose (Sun). Even though the picture on the card looks like an ending with all of the swords protruding from the corpse, the Sun is rising in the background[1].

If this card comes up in a reading, a difficult situation is over. There's nothing more to be done. Just let it go.

8.5 Pentacles

Page of Pentacles The Page of Pentacles is learning about creating material things, or could be some one about to take on a project.

Queen of Pentacles This Queen is a Capricorn, and therefore practical (Earth), focused (Saturn), and ambitious (Cardinal Earth). She has a good heart, though, even if she doesn't always know where it is.

---

[1] When looking into a Rider-Waite styled Tarot card, you are traditionally looking into the East.

King of Pentacles The King of Pentacles, as a Taurus, is also practical (Earth), but solid, and sometimes stubborn (Fixed). On the other hand, if you run into obstacles, he can get them cleared out for you in no time. The Venus influence on Taurus means that he'll also have the best stuff he can get.

Knight of Pentacles The Knight of Pentacles, as a Virgo, is the only Knight whose horse stands completely still. That might be because he's too busy thinking (Mercury) about all the details (Mutable Earth) of his next quest. There's no point in leaving until everything is just right.

Ace of Pentacles The Ace of Pentacles is a material beginning. You can think of it as a seed being planted, or a gift from the Universe that is in transit. It could also be saying that you need to start a project.

Two of Pentacles Jupiter in Capricorn, with the duality and alternation of Two. Capricorn's a Saturn-type place, so Jupiter's not really happy there, and there's more and more stuff to get together, but Jupiter doesn't really have the necessary focus.

The standard picture shows a young man holding pentacle in each hand. He is balancing or juggling the coins in front of a wavy sea in the background. If you see this card, you should ask if you've taken on more than you can handle.

Three of Pentacles Mars in Capricorn, with the growth and multiplication given by Three. The Saturn rulership of Capricorn gives focus and structure to the energy of Mars, which will help in getting things done.

The traditional meaning of this card is teamwork; craftsmanship is also implied. This card in a reading could be telling you to consult people you trust about a practical matter.

Four of Pentacles Sun in Capricorn, with the stability of Four. Capricorn can be miserly under stress (with some of the clinginess of its opposite, Cancer), and given that Earth signs are focused on the material, a little penny pinching is only natural.

This card is asking you if you are holding on to the right things. There may be something that you're holding on to that you need to let go of, or vice versa.

Five of Pentacles Mercury in Taurus, with the adjustment of Five. Under stress, Mercury in Taurus can mean a stubborn mind... too stubborn to ask for help when needed... even when walking in front of a church that could offer sanctuary... in the snow, barefoot.

If you see this card in a reading, you should examine your attitudes toward giving and receiving help.

Six of Pentacles Moon in Taurus, with the balance and harmony of Six. The moon (emotions) is well placed in Taurus (maintaining physical security), and focused on the Venus function of providing nice things for self and others, making sure everyone gets his due.

The traditional picture shows a rich man in the middle of the village square with an unfortunate on either side asking him for help. He is dispensing coins to one, and has a scale in his other hand. This card is asking whether your current allocation of resources is reasonable.

Seven of Pentacles Saturn in Taurus, with the expansive thought of Seven. Saturn is traditionally associated with delay, among other things, and Taurus with material comfort, but remember that Taurus is a Fixed Earth sign. The two together indicate growth, but gradual growth. If you see this card in a reading, and there's a situation that seems stagnant, you can assume that the expansion is actually taking place under the surface and will become apparent later.

Eight of Pentacles Sun in Virgo, with the move toward the concrete of Eight. The Sun in Virgo indicates that efficiency and attention to detail are tied in with identity. This is only increased by the concreteness of Eight.

The traditional meaning of this card is craftsmanship. Its message is: "Don't worry about results; just do the best you can and everything will work out."

Nine of Pentacles Venus in Virgo, with the completion of Nine. Traditional meanings are prosperity and refinement. Venus is unfortunately placed in Virgo, but the fullfillment and completion of the Nine make it all work out. The one downside is possible overattention to showy detail at the expense of substance.

Ten of Pentacles Mercury in Virgo, with the new cycle based on the Old of Ten. Mercury is at home in Virgo, and so is the family, along with a mysterious stranger that only the dogs seem to recognize.

If you see this card, it's clear that you've accomplished something, but you should start thinking about what you'd like to do next.

Chapter 9

The Major Arcana

The Major Arcana is a set of twenty-two cards, each with a different character portrayed. The cards normally indicate more important and even karmic matters in the course of a reading. The Major Arcana cards represent things that are inside you as well as things on the outside.

Each of the cards has a Number (except The Fool) and an astrological attribution. If the Number is greater than nine, it can be reduced to a Base Number, but the digits that comprise the Number have their own meanings. The astrological attribution can be either a Sign, a Planet, or an Element. As a starting point, we will say that the interpretation of each card involves a process described by the astrological attribution and working using a method described by the Number. In the cases where the number of the card is greater than nine, the process operates under the surface at first.

The Fool (0) The astrological attributions of the Fool are The Element Air and the Planet Uranus. The most basic meaning of the Element Air is change; similarly Uranus operates by making sudden or unexpected changes where necessary. So either way, let's say that the process of the Fool card is change.

Now let's look at the Number. You can't divide anything by zero, but the closer the number you're dividing by approaches zero, the larger the result gets. Similarly, the fewer possessions and commitments you have, the larger the number of possibilities available to you. Zero isn't a traditional number in Numerology, but for this purpose we can think of it as the Void from Taoism. It's a lot of nothing, but it's the origin of Everything.

The standard picture on the card is of a young man standing on a cliff with a dog. The man doesn't seem to notice the cliff and looks as though he is about to fall off. One interpretation I've seen is that the Fool represents the soul between lifetimes; he does step off the cliff, and lands in the maternity ward.

If you see this card in a reading, you may want to ask yourself if there's a cliff you need to step off of, or if you're heading toward a fall that can and should be avoided.

The Magician (I) The components of the Magician Card are the Number One and the Planet Mercury. Putting the two together yields a preliminary description: beginning to communicate with and learn from the immediate environment.

The Magician has a table in front of him, and on the table are a Wand, a Sword, a Cup and a Pentacle; in short, symbols of the Four Elements. If you are guessing that this shows he has control over the elements, you would be correct. This control is in the sense of the saying by Francis Bacon: "Nature, to be commanded, must be obeyed." The Magician is in control because he understands how things work. The Magician doesn't own the power, it just works through him.

In a reading, this card should prompt you to ask if you have more power available to you than you're aware of.

The High Priestess (II) The components of the High Priestess card are the Number Two and the Moon. The Number Two suggests communication and interaction, while the Moon suggests emotions. Also remember the Way of the High Priestess from Chapter 1. Putting the preceding together, we can conclude that the High Priestess also does magic, but in her own way. The High Priestess is the other side of the magical coin. The Magician does active magic driven by personal willpower, while functioning as a conduit for the Source. The High Priestess does passive magic driven by emotion. Her way is just as valid as the Magician's but is better suited for a different set of people.

The High Priestess sits calmly, with an almost smug expression on her face. The astrological attribution of the High Priestess is the Moon, so she also represents the subconscious and all of the processes that go on in life behind the scenes.

The High Priestess in a reading could be suggesting that you concentrate on how you'll feel when you get what you want, and let the Universe worry about the details.

The Empress (III) In interpreting the Empress card, we will use the Planet Venus and the Number Three. Venus is the Planet of nice things and people, and Three is about expansion and growth. The Empress creates new flowers in her garden, and is pregnant with her husband (The Emperor's) baby. She is the creative force of nature.

If you see the Empress in a reading, it's quite likely that something is growing for you as well. One of the traditional interpretations is that a baby may be on the way, but it could also refer to a creative work.

The Emperor (IV) The Emperor has the astrological attribution of the Sign Aries. Aries is the Cardinal Fire sign, and the Emperor is the result of the process of defining personal identity. Four is about stability, and combined with Aries in the Emperor, the identity definition is firm. The Emperor lays down the law in his kingdom, and decides how things will be done.

If you see the Emperor in a reading, you may be faced with a choice of what you want to have in your kingdom, or it may be a situation where you or someone else needs to lay down the law.

The Hierophant (V) The components of the Hierophant are the Number Five and the sign Taurus, which is a Fixed Earth Sign ruled by Venus. We'll start with the Sign: Fixed Earth translates to maintaining physical structure. Adding the Venus rulership indicates that the physical structure will be of above average quality. On the other hand, the Number Five indicates some destabilization.

We can resolve this apparent dilemma by assuming that it is our bad habits and improper beliefs that will be destabilized. Venus wants most to get along with everyone else, so this influence can lead you toward shared beliefs and conventional wisdom. In what areas of your life this may be necessary is a question for you to answer.

The Lovers (VI) The components of the Lovers are the Number Six and the Sign Gemini, which is a Mutable Air Sign ruled by Mercury. Mutable Air translates to evaluating thoughts and communication, and the Mercury influence emphasizes learning and communication. Six, on the other hand, symbolizes harmony and balance, so this card has a goal of harmony and balance through communication and evaluation.

Gemini is a Latin word meaning twins, and it's fitting that there are two popular versions of this card. The older version shows a man in the position of having to choose between two women of vastly different natures; the more modern version shows Adam and Eve in the Garden of Eden with an angel looking over them. So this card is at the same time about choice and about the interaction of the First Couple. Please note that Six is harmony and balance, but not stability. Equilibrium would be a more accurate description of Six's energy.

If you see this card in a reading, it doesn't necessarily mean a new or improved relationship; it could also just mean that you are or will be in a more peaceful state of mind than usual. Or it could mean that you have an important choice to make.

The Chariot (VII) The components of the Chariot are the Number Seven and the Sign Cancer, which is a Cardinal Water Sign ruled by the Moon. Seven indicates creating abstract concepts, while Cancer refers to the need to create emotional security, and the Moon symbolizes our emotions and habits. We could say, then, that the Chariot is actually constructed from our beliefs and habits that make us feel safe and in control.

The man in the traditional picture on this card looks a little like a crab in his shell. The traditional meaning of the Chariot is control through willpower. The two steeds represent the emotions; a weak man lets them drive, while a strong man has them under control. The Seven of the Chariot indicates creating abstract concepts from the safety of Six, which is mirrored by the driver's plate armor.

This card in a reading suggests two questions: first, "Is there an area of my life where I am trying too hard to feel like I'm in control?", and second, "Is there an area of my life where I'm letting my emotions run things?"

Strength (VIII) The components of Strength are the number Eight and the Sign Leo, which is a Fixed Fire Sign ruled by the Sun. The Number Eight refers to the process of making concrete examples of the concepts created by Seven. This means nailing things down, and therefore creating some stability. At the same time, the sign Leo as Fixed Fire translates to maintaining freedom and identity, while the Sun symbolizes identity and ego.

Strength is Leo, and the co-star of the card is a lion. The lion is being controlled by a woman who probably weighs 20 percent of what the lion does. This is obviously a different kind of control from the kind described by the Chariot. If you have the kind of control described by Strength, this control is based on the fact that you know and accept who you are. Which is better? It depends on the circumstances, but you actually need both.

If you see this card in a reading, it should prompt the question: "Is there something inside me which, though extremely powerful, is actually at peace and more than capable of enduring whatever may happen?"

The Hermit (IX) The Components of the Hermit are the number Nine and the Sign Virgo, which is a Mutable Earth Sign ruled by Mercury. Nine refers to completion of manifestation, and Mutable Earth translates to evaluating and communicating about physical things.

The Hermit is Virgo, and really performs the same function as the Vestal Virgins. To understand why, look at the picture on the card: the man stands on the top of a mountain, holding up a lantern. The lantern is for anyone who may be climbing the mountain, but the Hermit isn't really concerned about whether anyone is coming or not. The Nine of the Hermit is about completion and fulfillment. The Hermit has the whole story, and he's willing to share with whoever asks. If you see this card in a reading, you may want to ask if there's an area in your life where you may be needed to shed some light on the subject.

The Wheel of Fortune (X) The components of the Wheel are the Number One (reduced from ten) and the Planet Jupiter. One is the number of beginnings, but also unity. Jupiter symbolizes our urges for expansion and improvements, but also our need to believe in something larger than ourselves.

The Wheel is represented by Jupiter, which seems a bit odd on the surface, since the other connotation is fate, which one would expect to be associated with Saturn. One way of understanding this is that fate is a process, and if you trust in this process instead of fighting it, you can be like the sphinx who sits on top of the wheel and is unaffected by its motion.

The Wheel is the first of the Majors with a two-digit numbers. Two-digit numbers reduce to a Base Number by adding the digits together. What this means for us is that the qualities of the Base Number manifest, but after the qualities of the two-digit number. How two-digit numbers work before they are reduced is that the qualities of the first digit are active by way of the qualities of the second digit.

So the Wheel is One manifesting through Zero, or beginnings and initiative manifesting through the Great Void. This is the process that underlies the entire universe, so if the Wheel seems to be a fateful card, that's why.

If you see this card in a reading, ask yourself if there's an area of life where you need to trust the process and not try so hard for a particular result.

Justice (XI) The components of Justice are the number Two (reduced from eleven, or more accurately, two Ones) and the Sign Libra, which is the Cardinal Air Sign ruled by Venus. Associated with Two are alternation and interaction, even opposition. Cardinal Air translates to initiating communication and interaction, while the Venus (nice things and people) influence lends a desire for harmony.

Justice is represented by Libra, not the part of Libra that wants everyone to get along and have a good time, instead the part that wants balance and justice. There's no blindfold in the standard version of Justice, as this kind of justice isn't blind but instead sees all. The sword—and this is pretty much true in Tarot in general—is for cutting out things that no longer fit.

If you see this card in a reading, you should ask if there's an area of life that is out of balance or that needs some surgical incisions.

The Hanged Man (XII) The components of the Hanged Man are the Number Three (reduced from twelve) and the Element Water. Three is associated with growth and expansion, and also a resolution of the apparent conflict of Two. Water symbolizes emotions and emotional security.

The traditional picture is of a man hanging upside down from a tree over a river. The man has a serene expression, and there seems to be a glow around his head. He shows us emotional security in a seemingly insecure situation.

The Hanged Man is One working through Two, or initiative working through duality and alternation. The end result is the growth and multiplication of Three, but this watery growth that's unseen under the surface must complete first.

If you see this card in a reading, it just means that you need to hang out for a bit and be patient. Everything will be fine in the long run, even though you may be held up by opposition.

Death (XIII) The components of Death are the Number Four and the Sign Scorpio, which is the Fixed Water Sign ruled by Mars. One of the meanings of Four is stability, and Scorpio translates to maintaining emotional security. Mars, on the other hand, symbolizes our urges for self-assertion.

Death has the zodiac sign Scorpio for an attribution, and doesn't normally refer to physical death. It more often refers to a part of your life that is dying, or more precisely, either going away entirely, or changing to such an extent that it will no longer be recognizable after the change.

The number thirteen reduces to Four, the number of stability, and stability is what you will have after the process described above is finished. In the meantime, you have the growth and expansion of Three, as well as a planet that wants to be assertive struggling against a Sign that doesn't like change.

A good question to ask if you see this card in a reading is: "What area of my life needs a major change right now?"

Temperance (XIV) The components of Temperance are the Number Five and the Sign Sagittarius, which is the Mutable Fire Sign ruled by Jupiter. Five refers to destabilization and the breaking down of Four's structure, while Mutable Fire translates to evaluating freedom and identity, and Jupiter represents our urge for expansion and improvement. The combination points to an upcoming test. Testing is one of the meanings of the word "temper." The other meaning is "to balance" or "to moderate", which is one way of improving something found lacking.

The Ryder-Waite version shows an angel pouring water from one vessel into another, but there's an interesting version in the Builders of the Adytum deck: the angel is standing between an eagle and a lion. The angel is pouring water on the lion, and holding a torch above the eagle's head, thereby bringing water to fire and vice versa.

This is another case where the card is a precursor of the Number its digits add up to. Fourteen reduces to Five, the number of strife and stress. Temperance gives you a good base to stand on and face up to the stress. If you see this card, it's a good idea to ask if you may need to balance something in preparation for a test.

The Devil (XV) The components of the Devil are the Number Six and the Sign Capricorn, which is the Cardinal Earth Sign ruled by Saturn. Six is the number of balance and harmony, while Cardinal Earth translates to creating material security, and Saturn represents structure, limitation and focus. In the long run, the card points to balance and harmony with a sound basis, but there's an issue to resolve first.

The Devil is the "Father of Lies," and this card isn't really what it appears to be. For starters, compare it to the Lovers: both have Adam and Eve, a devil is really a fallen angel, and Fifteen reduces to Six. It's really the same scene, but after the Fall, when mankind becomes seduced by the material world (hence Capricorn, the Cardinal Earth sign).

The traditional meanings are bondage and addiction, but notice an important detail: the chains around Adam's and Eve's necks are not very tight. They could simply slip off the chains and walk away. If you see this card in a reading, ask yourself if you're not really tied to something as tightly as you think you are. That may be exactly the think you need to slip the chains off and walk away from.

The Tower (XVI) The components of the Tower are the Number Seven, which indicates development of abstract concepts, and the Planet Mars, which symbolizes our urge for self-assertion. Before the abstract concepts can be developed, a few things may need to be cleaned up.

The digits making up the base number are One (beginnings) and Six (balance and harmony). The balance and harmony will be temporarily out of service to implement the new beginning. Mars is in charge of this project.

The picture of the card seems to indicate the demolition of physical structures, but the meaning in practice of the card can be much scarier. The card most often indicates the demolition of belief systems. It heralds events that can make something you believe in impossible to believe in after that fact.

You can shortcut the process by asking what beliefs or habits you may have that no longer serve you.

The Star (XVII) The components of the Star are the Number Eight and the Sign Aquarius, which is the Fixed Air Sign ruled by Saturn. The Number Eight indicates creating concrete details of the abstract concepts created by Seven. Fixed Air translates to maintaining thoughts and communication.

In this context, the Star is one that you wish on. Your wish is fixed in your mind (Aquarius) until it comes true, or manifests in detailed concrete (Eight) form (Saturn).

If you see the Star in a reading, you should ask yourself if there's a source of hope or inspiration that you may not be aware of. Or make a wish.

The Moon (XVIII) The components of the Moon are the Number Nine and the Sign Pisces, which is the Mutable Water Sign ruled by Jupiter. The Number Nine indicates completion and fulfillment, while Mutable Water translates to evaluating emotional security, and Jupiter symbolizes the urge for expansion and improvement, as well as the need to believe in a higher being.

The components of the Moon are all positive, but the card itself is often regarded as scary, with interpretations including deception. This is really a matter of being afraid of the dark. Darkness and light in Tarot are metaphors. Things in daylight in Tarot card refer to things in your life that you are aware of, and things in darkness indicate things in your life that happen under the surface.

If you see the Moon in a reading, you should ask yourself if there's something you need to do that seems scary enough to cause you to procrastinate about it. When you think of the thing, remember that you don't have to be afraid of the dark any more.

The Sun (XIX) The components of the Sun are the Number One and the Sun[1]. The Number One indicates a beginning, but the individual digits of the card are One and Nine, so this

---

[1] Go figure!

beginning is based on the completion of prior work, and also relate to identity, which is what the Sun symbolizes.

It's instructive that the Number of this card reduces to the the Number of the Wheel of Fortune, which reduces to the Number of the Magician. I use the word "instructive" because the sequence is a good illustration of manifestation according to the Way of the Magician. Start with the good feelings you will have when the desired item is present or the desired event occurs. Next, let go of the item or event; you've specified What; let the Source worry about How. Finally, pay attention to the environment and look for the opportunity to use your tools to create the item or event.

If you see the Sun in a reading, you should ask yourself what would make you as happy as the child on the horse.

Judgement (XX) Judgement has the attribution of Fire, and the number Two working through Zero, or alternation and change working through the Void. Remember that Fire is about identity and freedom, and you can see how Judgement has the traditional meaning of "waking up" or becoming free of spiritual bondage.

If you see Judgement in a reading, ask yourself where in your life you may need to wake up and smell the coffee.

The World (XXI) The World has the attribution of Saturn, and the Number Two working through One, or alternation and change working through beginnings and initiative. All of this alternation and beginning has the structure of Saturn behind it, however, and the traditional meaning of the World is completion and fulfillment, but also the operation of the universe.

If you see the World in a reading, ask yourself what you may have accomplished that you haven't given yourself enough credit for.

Chapter 10

How to Do a Reading

10.1 Recipe for a Helpful Reading

The first ingredient for a successful reading is the cards. Tradition holds that a new Tarot reader should not buy a deck, but should receive it as a gift. If you've received a deck as a gift, consider yourself lucky, but it's by no means a requirement. Decks typically come with the cards perfectly ordered, starting with the Major Arcana, then the Minor Arcana arranged by Suit. Be sure to shuffle the deck thoroughly at least ten times. This will randomize the deck in preparation for future readings. Smudging the deck with sage smoke and sleeping with the deck under your pillow are strictly optional. If you plan to take your cards with you somewhere, an investment in either a cloth bag or wooden box to carry your cards in is recommended.

The next ingredient for a successful reading is you. You should be in a relatively quiet place where you will have a few minutes to yourself without being interrupted.[1] Take a few moments to relax and clear your mind of any worries or concerns. You want to have

---

[1] On the other hand, the author's favorite place to do Tarot readings for others is a local coffee shop.

an open-minded attitude and approach the reading as if you were meeting a new friend for the first time. If you find that you get distracted easily, you can visualize a bubble of light around yourself.

Next, we need a question. You can, of course, ask whatever question you want, but I have recommendations that will improve your results. The only person you can change or control is yourself, so questions about what you can do or about what you need to know are better than questions about why a certain other person is acting in a certain manner. In fact questions starting with the words "What do I need to know..." are the most productive of all.

Finally, we need a structure for the reading. It is entirely possible to draw one or many cards, intepreting each card individually, and I've seen readers who do just that. However, there are some benefits to using a predefined card layout, more commonly known as a spread among Tarot readers.

First, the most important ingredient in Tarot is your subconscious mind. The structure of a consistently applied layout will build itself into your subconscious. As a result, the more you work with a particular layout, the more consistent and pertinent your results will be.

Second, having a structured layout will allow the meanings of the card to vary in their application according to the position in the layout. These position-specific applications will then interact, creating themes and possibly highlighting larger issues.

In this chapter, we will be looking at a simple three-card spread and a more traditional spread called the Celtic Cross. You can use either of the spreads, or one of your own design or that you saw somewhere else. The important thing is that you decide on a spread before shuffling the cards.

If you have a particular topic that you're interested in, keep it in mind while shuffling, otherwise consider the question: "What do I most need to examine or address in my life at this moment?" Shuffle the cards at least seven times, or until you feel a comfort level that they are properly ordered for your question.

Now, cut the deck. I like to cut the deck into three piles, then put them back in reverse order, but it doesn't matter as long as you're consistent. Lay the cards out in the order given by your chosen spread. You can lay them out all face-up, or lay them out face-down and turn them over one at a time. Each reader develops their own personal relationship with Tarot, so it's important that you choose a method that you're comfortable with and that works for you.

The first spread is at the same time simple and versatile. You draw three cards: one for the past, one for the present, and one for the future. You can also vary the spread by assigning different sets of meanings. One example would be: problem, root cause, result. Or you could use one card for the body, one card for the mind, one card for the soul.

When reading the cards for yourself or others, remember that the set of interpretations I went over earlier is only a starting point. Over time, you may develop your own meanings for the cards, or at least your own insights about how the cards relate to your life. Another metaphor is that Tarot is a book which is written by its reader.

I recommend using this simple spread for the first few readings. You can then move on to the Celtic Cross if you wish, or another spread of your choice.

10.2 The Celtic Cross

The Celtic Cross is a spread of ten cards, set up in two sections. The section on the left resembles a cross, and to the right is a column of four cards resembling a staff. The ten cards are assigned different roles according to their position in the spread. There are different systems of assigning the roles, so if you see them assigned differently in another book, don't be alarmed. Like anything in Tarot, you'll need to decide on a system that works best for you.

1. This card describes an aspect of the current situation.

Figure 10.1: The Celtic Cross Spread

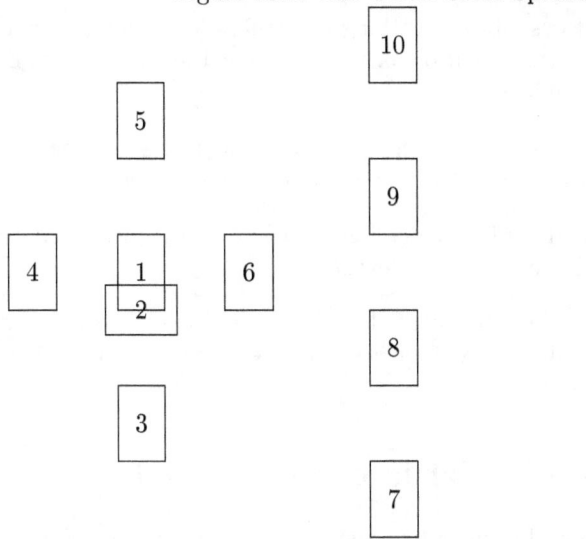

2. This card describes a factor that could make the current situation either easier or more difficult.

3. This card could describe a root cause of the situation, or an influence that exists under the surface.

4. This card describes either a past influence, or an influence that has outlived its usefulness and should be let go of.

5. This card could describe a possible goal, or an inflence that is already known.

6. This card describes a future influence, or something present now that could influence the future.

7. This card describes something about how you see yourself in this situation, or what to do about the situation on a physical

level.

8. This card describes something about how you see your environment in this situation, or what to do on the level of thought and communication.

9. This card describes something about your hopes and fears in this situation, or what to do on an emotional level.

10. This card describes a possible outcome of the situation, or what to do on a spiritual level.

In summary, the first six cards describe the current situation and its influences, and the next four describe how you may feel about it and what to do.

10.3 Sample Celtic Cross Spread

As an illustration, I'm including a spread I did for myself recently, along with my interpretation of it.

1. The World. This card suggests completion and fulfillment, so naturally the question is "What currently makes me feel complete and fulfilled?"

2. Knight of Wands. This card suggests the flamboyant and adventurous Sagittarius. I'm sure this Knight wants everyone to know about the World being my first card. So an appropriate question is: "How can I best let everyone know about what I've learned and accomplished?"

3. The Magician. This card suggests power and control over the elements, but its position indicates that it's under the surface. This leads me to ask: "Is it possible that I have more power and control in my current situation than I may consciously realize?"

4. The Chariot. This card suggests control by willpower, as opposed to letting the universe work through me as the Magician does. Its position in the past leads me to ask: "What am I currently trying to consciously assert control over that I need to let go of and hand off to the universe to take care of?"

5. The Page of Swords is learning about honesty, truth and justice. It's position as a highest goal leads me to ask: "In what areas of my life do I need to start thinking about honesty, truth and justice?"

6. The Five of Cups suggests disappointment and regret. It's in the near future position. I could read this card as saying disappointment and regret are waiting for me, but a more empowering interpretation is that there's already something in my life that I'm disappointed about or regret, and that I'll need to face up to that at some point in the near future. Or I can think about it and face up to it now.

7. The Knight of Pentacles is a reliable, detail-oriented Virgo, in the position of self, or physical action item. This leads me to ask: "Where can I set things in order with my attention to detail?"

8. The Five of Swords suggests unnecessary competitiveness, to the point of seeking to impose defeat. In the position of others, or mental action item, it leads me to ask: "Where am I drawing my sword unnecessarily? Would I rather be right or happy?"

9. The Five of Pentacles suggests hardship, but unnecessary hardship in the sense that help is avaliable if requested. In the position of hopes and fears, or emotional action item, it leads me to ask: "Where in my emotional life do I feel needy? Do I have resources in this area that I am not utilizing?"

10. The High Priestess suggests an inner knowing and a passive magic. In the position of final outcome, or spiritual action

item, it leads me to ask: "About what should I be wishing to the moon instead of striving for?"

As you can see, just one reading can generate a lot of things to think about. I recommend doing at least one reading a month for yourself, but not more than one per week. On the other hand, it is also a good practice to pick a daily card and relate it to the day's events. This is a good way to study each card in more detail and develop a more personal interpretation.

10.4 Reading for Others

As you become more familiar with Tarot, it is only natural for you to want to share its benefits with others, and maybe even make a career out of it.

The most important element in reading for others is trust. The person you're doing the reading for needs to trust you, of course, but the need goes further down than you think. Without the trust, you not only won't be able to do a good reading, but the cards themselves will be closed off from the other person[2]. Also, you need to trust the cards, and, most importantly, yourself.

The next thing is the card interpretations. Naturally, you'll have developed your own personal set of meanings while doing readings for yourself. These meanings will vary from reader to reader. If the querent (which is a fancy name for the person you're reading for) has been to other readers, he will most likely have been exposed to some card meanings that differ from yours. The querent may even have his own ideas about the cards based on the artwork. This is actually a good thing, because the whole goal of a reading is to get inside the querent's head and pull out some things that may be helpful. So feel free to ask during the course of the reading if the querent has any thoughts about the cards that appear.

---

[2] The author found this out the hard way when he did his first paid reading.

Finally, don't feel that you have to provide definitive answers to the querent or solve his problems. You are not the Delphic Oracle[3]. Your responsibility in doing a reading for someone else is to ask the right questions, and get the querent thinking differently in some way.

---

[3] and no one listened to the Oracle anyway

Bibliography

[1] Bernadette Brady, *Predictive Astrology: The Eagle and the Lark*, Weiser Books, 1998.

[2] Demetra George, *Astrology and the Authentic Self: Integrating Traditional and Modern Astrology to Uncover the Essence of the Birth Chart*, Ibis Press, Florida, 2008.

[3] Kay Lagerquist, Ph.D. and Lisa Lenard, *The Complete Idiot's Guide to Numerology*, Alpha, 2004.

[4] Gahl Sasson, *Cosmic Navigator: Design Your Destiny with Astrology and Kabbalah*, Red Wheel/Weiser, 2008.

[5] Jan Spiller, *New Moon Astrology: The Secret of Astrological Timing to Make All Your Dreams Come True*, Bantam Dell, New York, 2001.

www.ingramcontent.com/pod-product-compliance
Lightning Source LLC
LaVergne TN
LVHW051134080426
835510LV00018B/2413